Famous Battles of the Age of Revolution

Chris McNab

Cavendish Square
New York

This edition published in 2018 by Cavendish Square Publishing, LLC
243 5th Avenue, Suite 136, New York, NY 10016

First Edition

Cataloging-in-Publication Data

Names: McNab, Chris.
Title: Famous battles of the age of revolution / Chris McNab.
Description: New York : Cavendish Square Publishing, 2018. | Series: Classic warfare | Includes bibliographical references and index.
Identifiers: ISBN 9781502632524 (library bound)
Subjects: LCSH: Revolutions--History--Juvenile literature.
Classification: LCC D21.3 M37 2018 | DDC 909—dc23

Editorial Director: David McNamara
Editor: Michael Sciandra
Associate Art Director: Amy Greenan
Production Coordinator: Karol Szymczuk

Printed in the United States of America

The photographs in this book are used by permission and through the courtesy of: AKG Images: 7 bottom (Peter Connolly), 16 (Erich Lessing), 30–31 (Maximilianeum Collection), 36 (Peter Connolly), 64–65, 72 (Coll. Archiv F. Kunst & Geschichte), 74 (Cameraphoto), 81 (Coll. Archiv F. Kunst & Geschichte), 86–87, 89 (Westfaelisches Schulmuseum), 90–91 (Bibliotheque Nationale), 108 (World History Archive), 111 (Bibliotheque Nationale), 126 (Cameraphoto), 128–129 (Cameraphoto), 140 (Coll. Archiv F. Kunst & Geschichte), 156 (British Library), 168 (Coll. Archiv F. Kunst & Geschichte), 172–173 (Erich Lessing), 179 (Visioars), 180–181 (Jerome da Cunha), 196–197 (Erich Lessing), 198 (IAM), 244 (Coll. Archiv F. Kunst & Geschichte), 270; Alamy: 48–49 (North Wind Picture Archives), 52 (Art Directors & TRIP), 104 (North Wind Picture Archives), 118 (Art Archive), 132 (Classic Images), 154 (Timewatch Images), 164–165 (Art Archive), 178 (Classic Image), 222 (Art Gallery Collection), 272–273 (Art Archive), 278–279 (Art Archive), 300–301 (Art Archive); Amber Books: 6, 7 top; Art Archive: 120–121 (National Museum Damascus/Gianni Dagli Orti), 146–147 (Pharonic Village, Cairo/Gianni Dagli Orti), 264–265 (Musée du Château de Versailles/Gianni Dagli Orti); Art-Tech/MARS: 276, 288, 295, 312; Bibliotheque Nationale de France: 102; Bridgeman Art Library: 18–19 (Look & Learn), 26, 38–39 (Giraudon), 40 (Alinari), 56 (Anne van Biema Collection), 117 (Giraudon), 170 (Agra Art), 182 (Archives Charmet), 202 (Giraudon), 208–209 (Society of Apothecaries), 227 (Maidstone Museum & Art Gallery), 234–235 (National Army Museum), 238 (Pushkin Museum), 240–241, 250–251, 254–255 (Stapleton Collection), 282 (Galleria d'Arte Moderna), 286–287 (Mansell Collection), 292–293 (Stapleton Collection), 296 & 297 (National Army Museum), 306, 308–309 (State Central Artillery Museum), 311 (National Army Museum); Corbis: 8–9 (Historical Picture Archive), 10 (Richard T. Nowitz), 13 (Jose Fuste Raga), 14 (Sandro Vannini), 44 (Bettmann), 50 (Araldo de Luca), 76 (Richard T. Nowitz), 96–97 (Stefano Bianchetti), 142 (Bettmann), 188–189 (Art Archive/Alfredo Dagli Orti), 200 (Araldo de Luca), 204 (Asian Art Archaeology), 210 (Reuters/Kim Kyung-Hoon), 216 (Werner Forman); De Agostini: 42; Mary Evans Picture Library: 28 (Edwin Mullan Collection), 34, 63, 68, 82, 122, 138, 163, 174, 220, 232, 236; Getty Images: 20 (Superstock), 54 (Hulton Archive), 98 (Hulton Archive); Library of Congress: 256, 257, 258, 304; Malta Tourist Authority: 152; Photos.com: 92, 100, 160, 206, 230, 262, 278; Photo12.com: 41 (Oronoz), 136–137 (Anne Ronan Picture Library), 158–159 (Bibliotheque Nationale), 162 (Hachette), 186 (EUK-Opid), 215 (JTB Photo); Leven Smits Creative Commons Licence: 114–115; TopFoto: 58 (Granger Collection), 246 (Ullsteinbild), 298 (RIA Novosti); Werner Forman Archive: 218–219 (Kuroada Collection); All maps © Amber Books.

Contents

The Wars of the Revolution

The battles of the Revolutionary period are dominated by those of the American War of Independence and the wars fought by the various European coalitions against the armies of Napoleonic France. The American battles were small scale—colonial militia pitting their wits and pluck against the British redcoats, exploiting the gaps in their drawn-out chains of command and unfamiliarity with the local terrain.

Napoleon Bonaparte may have been a megalomaniac who roused practically a whole continent to take up arms against him, but he was also a great soldier, respected by his men as one of their own. Some of his finest victories included Austerlitz (1805), but it must be placed against the folly of the ignominious retreat from Moscow (1812). Some of the most pitiless of battles were fought in this period. The French lost 25,000 men and the Prussians 15,000 at Eylau (1807). "What a massacre!" exclaimed a forlorn Marshal Ney, contemplating the dreadful scene. "And without a result!"

◀ **1801 Copenhagen — Nelson's grimly-fought battle with the Danes, more intense even than the fighting at Trafalgar, eventually saw an armistice signed and the legend of Nelson firmly established.**

Bunker Hill 1775

KEY FACTS

WHO	British troops under General William Howe against the American militia under overall command of Colonel William Prescott.
WHAT	The British launched several determined attempts to break hastily assembled American fortifications on the Charlestown peninsula. They finally succeeded, but at a heavy cost in terms of casualties.
WHERE	Charlestown, Massachusetts.
WHEN	June 17, 1775
WHY	The Americans had laid siege to the port of Boston at an early stage of the War of Independence.
OUTCOME	The British would continue to find themselves hemmed in on several fronts, and Howe would eventually have to evacuate Boston.

Ever since the Boston Tea Party in 1773, in which the colonials tipped British tea into the harbor as a furious gesture against taxes imposed by the British government, Boston had been at the heart of rising tensions. They were to burst aflame at the Battle of Bunker Hill.

AMERICAN WAR OF INDEPENDENCE

BRITISH VICTORY

The American War of Independence seemed made for the creation of heroes, as local militia from the colonies confronted the imperial might of the British army.

LOCATION

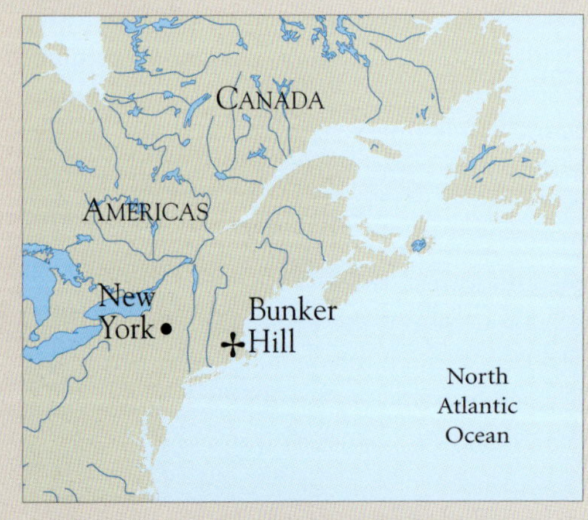

Bunker Hill, on the peninsula of Charlestown, was on obvious position from which to adopt a defensive or offensive position on the Boston port.

At an early stage in the American War of Independence, the British army had found itself under siege at Boston. As the American militia gradually entrenched themselves in the surrounding countryside, a plan had been hatched by the British commander General Thomas Gage to gain control of the Charlestown peninsula across the harbor to facilitate a lifting of the blockade. American militia beat him to it, however, rapidly moving in to take control of Bunker Hill and Breed's Hill on the peninsula, and speedily erecting a redoubt upon the latter, from which artillery fire could be more readily directed on Boston.

General William Howe, one of a group of generals sent from London to assist Gage in breaking the siege, was assigned to attack the American positions. He began by landing with his men on the south easternmost shore of the peninsula at Moulton's Point. On arrival, he spotted that the Americans had further troop reinforcements on Bunker Hill, so he sent word back to the mainland to be supplied further soldiers. By then sitting back and waiting for these reinforcements to arrive, Howe lost valuable

The Americans' siege of Boston came at an early stage of the War of Independence. Although the British would manage to lift the siege, they sustained heavy losses, and the rebels struck an early blow to their morale and future offensive capabilities.

momentum, for at this stage,the American troops had still not been fully deployed around their fortifications.

By mid-afternoon, the British reinforcements had arrived. A force under Brigadier General Robert Pigot began a feinted attack from the left flank on the redoubt, but as it did so it came under heavy sniper fire from the village of Charlestown. Howe now requested that Admiral Samuel Graves, whose boats had been ferrying the British soldiers across the bay, provided support fire. In the process of this, the village was set ablaze, by which time Pigot had pulled back. Howe had also launched an attack on the American left, but as the militia held their ground, he was forced to fall back under an onslaught of heavy artillery fire.

The British regrouped, this time planning for Pigot to launch a full attack on the redoubt while Howe led another assault on the American left. Once again, neither attack was successful, and the British were driven back under heavy fire, some of the companies so badly hit that they were reduced to single figures.

Howe now sent a message back to Boston requesting further soldiers, while persuading a number of those among his wounded to gird themselves for further action. But the Americans commanders were not without their problems either, with several companies beginning to retreat from the fortifications. One such company was brought back into line only when a neighboring company under Captain John Chester from Connecticut turned and aimed their muskets at them, forcing them to reconsider.

Howe's final attack was made directly on the redoubt, and with the Americans now beginning to run short of ammunitions, they were able to break through. Once inside the redoubt, the battle turned into hand-to-hand fighting in which the British, with their bayonets, were at an advantage.

The Americans were eventually forced off the peninsula, and the British able to fortify Bunker Hill and Breed's Hill. But the cost had been disproportionately high. They had lost twice as many men as the Americans—40 percent of their attacking force—and this was not only a blow to morale but would also hinder their capability for future offensives.

Saratoga 1777

The Americans had been lobbying the French for some time for more support in their quest for independence. The resilience and professionalism shown by their army against the British at Saratoga finally induced the French to fully commit to the cause.

AMERICAN WAR OF INDEPENDENCE

AMERICAN VICTORY

KEY FACTS

Who British troops under General John Burgoyne against the Americans under General Horatio Gates.

What The British general John Burgoyne found his advance on Albany blocked by American troops, and attempted to storm his way through by attacking their fortifications near Saratoga. His outnumbered forces were convincingly repulsed.

Where Saratoga County, New York.

When September 19, and October 7, 1777

Why The British were trying to take New York, which was a stronghold in the American battle for independence.

Outcome The American cause was taken increasingly seriously by the French after their victory at Saratoga, and they would soon form an alliance.

For General John Burgoyne, an imaginative but somewhat headstrong commander, surrender to Horatio Gates at Saratoga represented a huge personal blow.

LOCATION

Saratoga, north of Albany, was key to the British campaign to gain the upper hand in New York and the Hudson River.

The British strategy in the US War of Independence placed great importance on subduing New York, an area where it had encountered fiercest resistance. General John Burgoyne understood that gaining control of the valley of the Hudson River and the regional capital Albany was vital, but while he was successful when operating along the waterway, movement over ground proved trickier in an area that had few roads, and which was often blocked by trees felled to slow the progress of British troops. When Burgoyne reached Saratoga, north of Albany, things began to go seriously awry.

Part of the plan involved a force of 1000 men under the command of Barry St. Leger joining up with Burgoyne in Albany, having first gained control of central New York. But St. Leger's column relied heavily on Indian recruits, and these had a reputation for unreliability. When news reached them of the approach of an American force heading towards them to relieve St. Leger's siege of Fort Stanwix, they deserted, and St. Leger, finding himself in danger of being trapped by a much larger army, had no

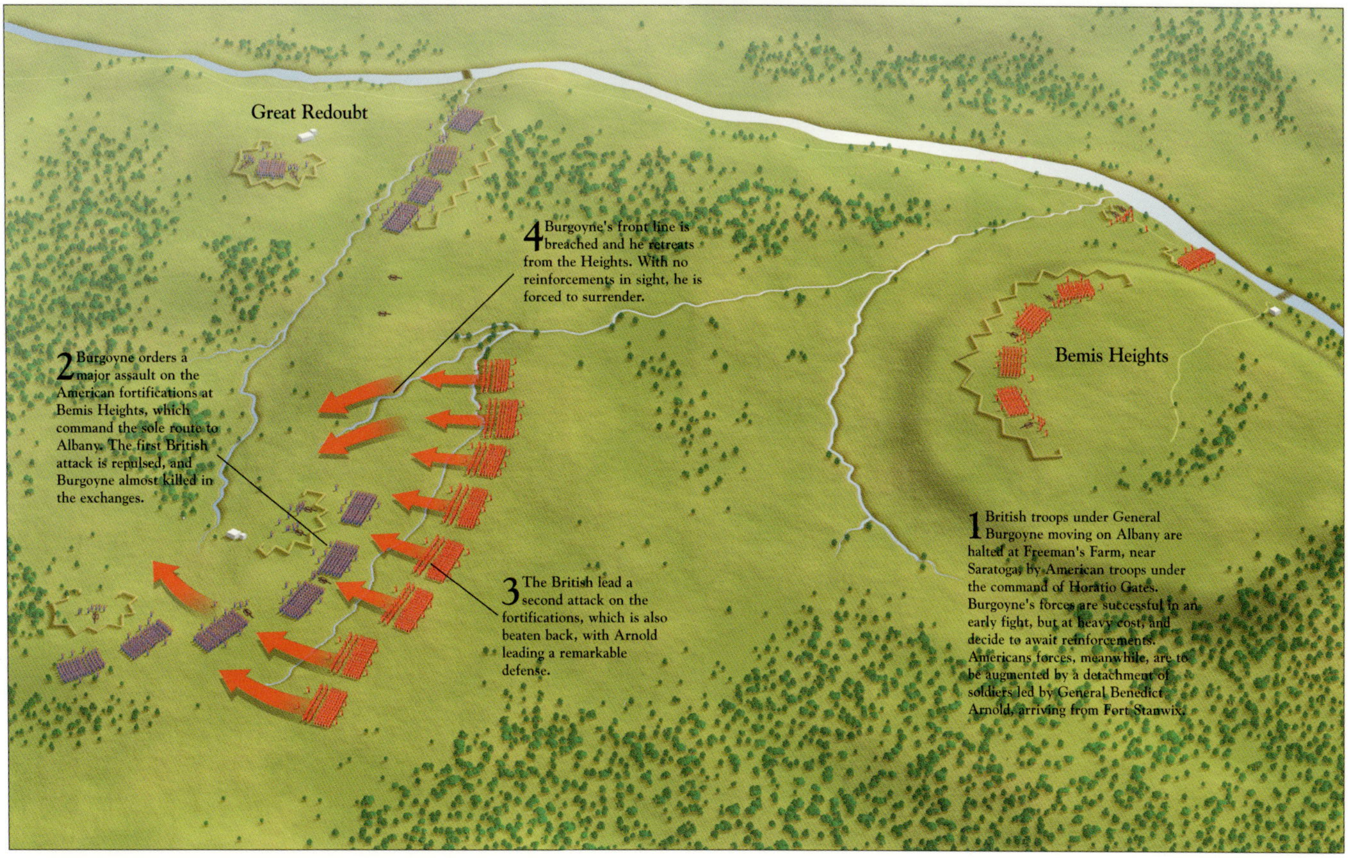

The British defeat at the Battle of Saratoga put a major dent in British pride and confidence in North America. In the two battles around Saratoga, the British lost a total of around 1000 men, against 500 casualties on the American side.

choice but to retreat into Canada, effectively taking himself out of the New York campaign.

Next Burgoyne ran into difficulties at Saratoga. German mercenaries in his employ went out scouting for supplies, but their haughty manner prompted many hitherto neutral locals to throw in their lot with the rebels. His Indians soldiers didn't help either by scalping a local woman, Jane McCrea. Even though she was married to a loyalist in Burgoyne's army, the failure to punish those Indians responsible made her a local cause célèbre, and another rallying point for the American rebels.

SEPTEMBER BATTLE

The first Battle of Saratoga took place at Freeman's Farm, after the arrival of American troops led by Horatio Gates, dispatched from Virginia by George Washington to halt Burgoyne's movement on Albany. The clash was won by the British, but as it came with the loss of a considerable number of men, Burgoyne decided to sit tight and await further reinforcements. However, it was the Americans whose numbers were to be augmented, in the shape of the detachment of soldiers led by General Benedict Arnold from Fort Stanwix.

Fearing winter could soon close in, and with sign of relief soldiers on the horizon, Burgoyne ordered a major assault on Bemis Heights, where the Americans had taken up a fortified position, commanding the only route to Albany. Although the rebels had the advantage of position, there were deep divisions within their command structure on the arrival of Arnold, to the extent that Gates had actually removed Arnold from field command.

The first British attack on the American defenses was repulsed, with Burgoyne almost losing his life. The second also failed, and was notable for a remarkable appearance by Arnold. Seemingly in a state of considerable agitation, he disobeyed orders and rode into the fray, leading the defense of the American redoubts that the British were attempting to capture. The attack having failed, and with his front line breached, Burgoyne had little option but to retreat. Increasingly surrounded and outnumbered, he would soon surrender to the Americans, for whom victory at Saratoga was seen as a turning point in their cause.

TIMELINE

1500–1000BC	1000–500BC	500BC–0AD	0–500AD	500–1000AD	1000–1500AD	1500–2000AD

Paulus Hook 1779

KEY FACTS

WHO "Light Horse Harry" (Major Henry) Lee led the American Continental Army against British and Loyalist forces in charge of the fort at Paulus Hook.

WHAT Lee led a successful raid on an isolated British- and Loyalist-held fort at an important control point on the Hudson River.

WHERE Paulus Hook, New Jersey.

WHEN August 19, 1779

WHY The British had a firm grip on New York, underpinned by naval control of the Hudson and the fortresses alongside it.

OUTCOME The British retained the fort, but many of their soldiers were taken prisoner, and Lee was acclaimed by George Washington and honored as a hero.

AMERICAN WAR OF INDEPENDENCE

AMERICAN VICTORY

The American War of Independence made heroes of many men, one of whom was the distinguished cavalryman from Virginia, "Light Horse Harry" Lee. But when he led an impudent night-time raid on the important fort at Paulus Hook in 1779, the British were distinctly unamused.

The British seemingly did not hear "Light Horse Harry" Lee's approaching army. Despite a few of his men getting lost in the woods, Lee was able to bring off one of the most daring escapades of the American War of Independence.

The British grip on New York, won at a staggering cost to the Americans in a series of battles in late 1776, remained a hindrance and a threat to the American Continental cause until the final British withdrawal in November of 1783. British vessels of war prowled up the Hudson as far as the great American bastion of West Point, while soldiers and supplies took advantage of Manhattan's superb harbor and transportation system. Neither Washington nor his subordinate commanders were willing to leave matters as they stood. The isolated British and Loyalist bastion across the Hudson at Paulus Hook allowed the British to control access to the river, but it also offered an inviting target.

A "BRILLIANT" ATTACK

"Light Horse Harry" Lee launched a nocturnal raid on the outpost, leading his men stealthily through approach woods, intending to set fire to the fort's barracks. Finding it occupied by sick soldiers and civilians, he instead carried off 159 rebel prisoners. George Washington described Lee's attack as a "brilliant" success. The British were considerably unnerved by this audacious escapade into the very heart of their defenses.

LOCATION

The vast fjord made by the Hudson River into the heart of eastern North America was perhaps the most vital waterway of the American War of Independence.

TIMELINE

1500–1000BC	1000–500BC	500BC–0AD	0–500AD	500–1000AD	1000–1500AD	1500–2000AD

Guilford Courthouse 1781

KEY FACTS

Who General Lord Cornwallis leads the British forces against Americans under General Nathanael Greene.

What Cornwallis had made camp to rest his tired troops, when reports came that Greene's men were also encamped nearby. He seized upon the moment to attack.

Where Modern-day Greensboro, Guilford County, North Carolina.

When March 15, 1781

Why The British were engaged in a bitter war in the southern colonies. The appointment of Greene buoyed the Americans, yet the British looked like they were in a position to nail their advantage in the south.

Outcome Cornwallis was able to drive the Americans off, but lost a quarter of his men, forcing him to withdraw.

In 1781, Lord Cornwallis's British army was sick and weary and suffering from desertions. Despite this, when he learnt of the presence of the enemy near Guilford Courthouse, he could not resist the urge to engage in battle. Technically, he won, but at considerable cost to his troops and British strategy.

AMERICAN WAR OF INDEPENDENCE

BRITISH VICTORY

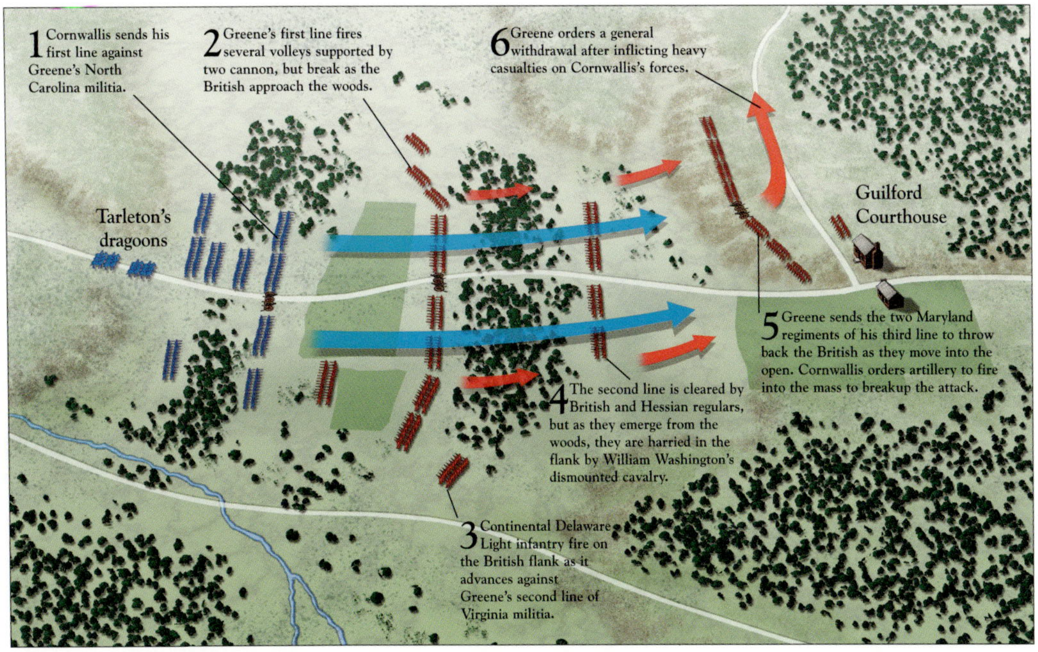

Guilford Courthouse was really a battle Cornwallis and the British could have done without. They won in the end, but the tricky terrain, with plenty of woodland cover, provided plenty of opportunities to ensnare them with artillery fire.

LOCATION

The British campaign in the southern colonies was designed to break the stalemate that had developed in the north.

The British hoped that fighting in the south would draw the southern colonies firmly behind them, and ultimately help break the stalemate in the north. But when General Nathaniel Greene was appointed the new commander of the American forces, he was able to assemble an army twice the size of that under Lord Cornwallis, and waged a war of attrition.

HOLLOW VICTORY

The gradual erosion of British forces took its toll, and Cornwallis had withdrawn to make camp at Hillsbororough, North Carolina, when he received news that Greene's men were themselves camped not far away. Cornwallis decided to give battle and, despite coming under heavy fire from American guns whose range was longer than those of his own, managed to drive the Americans from the field. But in doing so he lost half of the 1900 men he had at his disposal during the engagement. He now had to abandon his campaign in Carolina, withdrawing to Wilmington to rest and re-supply, before marching north into Virginia, where he was later besieged at Yorktown.

TIMELINE

1500–1000BC	1000–500BC	500BC–0AD	0–500AD	500–1000AD	1000–1500AD	1500–2000AD

Yorktown 1781

AMERICAN WAR OF INDEPENDENCE

FRANCO-AMERICAN VICTORY

KEY FACTS

WHO A British army of 8000 men under Major-General Charles Cornwallis (1738–1805), opposed by a 17,000-strong Franco-American army under Lieutenant-General George Washington (1732–99) and Lieutenant-General Jean-Baptiste de Rochambeau (1725–1807).

WHAT Cornwallis advanced into Virginia without orders, placing his force in a compromising position. He then retreated to Yorktown, where he was besieged.

WHERE Yorktown, on the York River in Virginia.

WHEN September 28–October 19, 1781

WHY Cornwallis believed that an advance into Virginia would improve the British hold on the southern states.

OUTCOME The British army was forced to surrender, convincing Parliament that the war in the colonies could not be won.

After realizing that advancing into Virginia was a mistake, the British had withdrawn to the coast—the right decision had the Royal Navy enjoyed its usual supremacy at sea. But French naval forces were able to blockade Yorktown, cutting off supplies and troop reinforcements.

The British forces' surrender at Yorktown came after an attempt by Major-General Charles Cornwallis to break out across the river was thwarted by bad weather.

LOCATION

The Virginia Peninsula offered the British the chance to develop a secure base, but instead it turned into a trap when control of the sea lanes was lost.

Despite winning battles, the British had failed to achieve victory in the north, and so transferred troops southwards to seek a decisive action there. Clearing the Carolinas of regular enemy forces, Cornwallis made the fateful decision to advance into Virginia, eventually marching to Yorktown, on Chesapeake Bay.

The British war effort in America depended upon sea links for communication, resupply and the movement of reinforcements, so a position on the coast made strategic sense. Dominance of the seas around North America was taken almost for granted. Certainly there was nothing that the American colonists could do to challenge the Royal Navy. However, the same was not true of the French navy, and a failure to intercept their ships aided the Franco-American strategic position. The French were also able to bring in reinforcements and artillery to be used in the siege of Yorktown, which began on September 28, in a combined effort of the Franco-American army under George Washington and the French commander General de Rochambeau.

The British forces attempted to dig in at Yorktown, while they also attempted to retain control of the sea. Despite doughty resistance, the combined forces of the Americans and French would force their eventual surrender.

Cornwallis was dismayed at his predicament, but ensured a system of defenses and outworks were put in position and manned. Yorktown was defended by seven main redoubts, with artillery batteries covering the river narrows as well. An inner line of earthworks protected the town itself.

The British were already short of food, and now slaughtered a large proportion of their horses to avoid having to feed them. Enough were retained to allow a foraging party of cavalry to be sent out on October 3, but this force was chased back into the siege lines, which continued to tighten as the besiegers began work on a trench parallel to the defenses.

The defenders' artillery positions came under fire from heavier and more numerous guns in the Franco-American siege train. The barrage covered the digging of a second parallel (a system of trenches), much closer to the defense lines. This was ready by October 12, though it was not a complete encirclement because two British-held redoubts blocked the path to the river. These were named Redoubts 9 and 10 by the British.

As work continued to construct trenches ever closer to the British lines, Washington planned an assault on the outlying redoubts. These were blasted with artillery for an extended period, but were still formidable when the assault went in. The French attack on Redoubt 9 was held up by abatis, large obstructions constructed of wood with spikes or blades sticking out. The French were challenged and then fired on as they began their assault, but were able to break through. The American force took Redoubt 10 after a ferocious bayonet fight that finally overwhelmed the defenders.

With the redoubts lost, Yorktown came under artillery fire from three directions. It was clear that the defenders could not hold out much longer unless the artillery bombardment was slackened. A few British soldiers did manage to get across the York River in a desperate escape plan by Cornwallis, but bad weather prevented a mass break-out. With more artillery being moved into position by the besiegers, the military situation in Yorktown was completely hopeless. On October 19, the British force finally surrendered.

TIMELINE

1500–1000BC	1000–500BC	500BC–0AD	0–500AD	500–1000AD	1000–1500AD	1500–2000AD

Yorktown

YORKTOWN

When General Cornwallis's cornered British army surrendered at Yorktown to the Americans in 1781, news filtered back to England. Lord North, the prime minster, cried out, "Oh God! It is all over." He knew that the attempt to the thwart the American fight for independence was finally lost. Victory had been achieved thanks to a massive artillery bombardment and the successful storming of the redoubts from which the British had attempted to defend their positions. It was the biggest humiliation yet suffered by the British army.

Karansebes 1788

KEY FACTS

WHO Hussars of the Austrian army and their fellow infantry inadvertently fire on each other.

WHAT Panic had broken out in an Austrian camp. Thinking they were about to be attacked by Turks, and in fading light, the Austrians began defending themselves against what, as it turned out, were their own comrades.

WHERE Karansebes, now Caransebes, in modern Romania.

WHEN 1788

WHY The Hapsburgs had made an alliance with Russia against the Ottoman Turks.

OUTCOME The Turks arrived on the scene some time later to discover 10,000 dead or maimed Austrian soldiers.

Joseph II was a ruler with "advanced" ideas on the role of the monarch, in sharp contrast to his reactionary mother, the Empress Marie Theresa. He wasn't a great fighting man, though, and the farce of Karansebes, assuming it really occurred, would have added no feathers to his cap.

AUSTRO-TURKISH WAR

TURKISH VICTORY

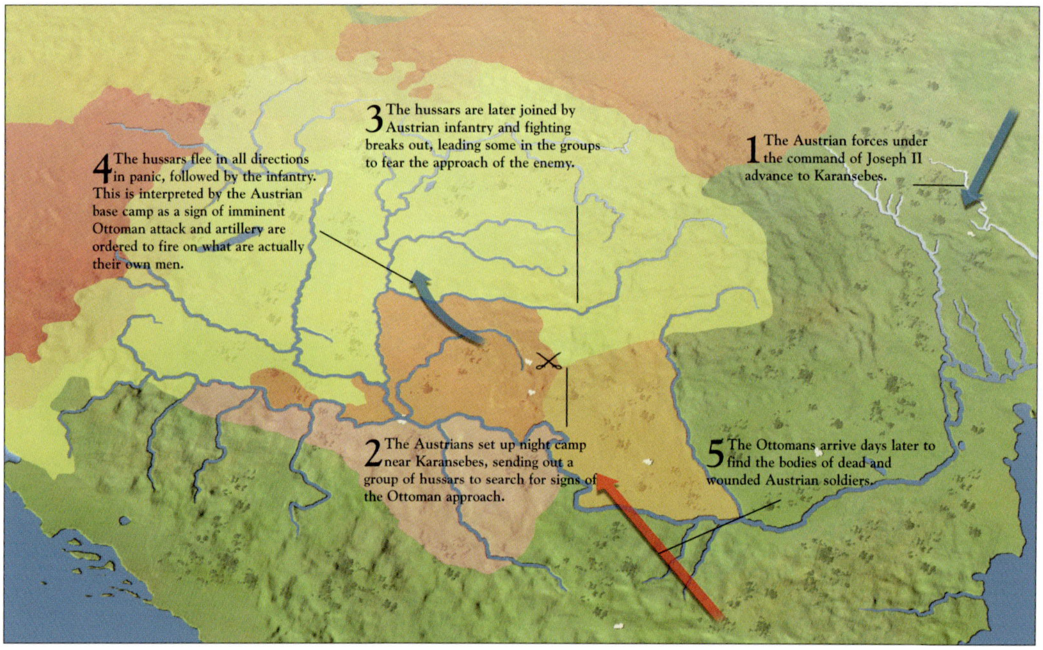

The Battle of Karansebes is one of the most excessive examples of "friendly fire" in history. The battle was fought and "lost" by the Austrians without the enemy even making an appearance.

Of all the unlikely episodes in military history, the farce of Karansebes takes the gold star. So incredible were the events, in fact, that many doubt that it ever happened—and with good reason, as the first account of the "battle" was not written up until half a century after it allegedly occurred.

Austria had declared war on the Ottoman Turks. Emperor Joseph II, no great shakes as a general, led the troops on the front line. His army had set up a night camp near Karansebes, when, so the story goes, hussars were sent out to check for any sign of the enemy. They were later joined by some infantry and a scuffle seems to have broken out over alcohol, leading one infantryman to cry out in jest, "Turks! Turks!" His fellow soldiers—many of different nationalities, a fact that underscores the potential for misunderstanding—failed to see the joke. The hussars panicked and fled in all directions, followed by many of the infantry. Back at base camp, an officer interpreted it as a sign of imminent Ottoman attack and ordered his artillery to fire. When the Ottomans did arrive, a couple of days later, all they found were thousands of dead and wounded Austrian soldiers.

LOCATION

Karansebes lies in modern Romania. In the eighteenth century it was part of the Austrian empire and viewed as conquerable territory by the Ottomans.

TIMELINE

1500–1000BC	1000–500BC	500BC–0AD	0–500AD	500–1000AD	1000–1500AD	1500–2000AD

Svensksund 1790

KEY FACTS

WHO A Swedish flotilla under the personal command of King Gustavus III of Sweden against a Russian fleet led by its commander Prince Charles von Nassau-Siegen.

WHAT The Russians underestimated the strength of the fleet they were attacking, and lost almost 10,000 men and nearly 90 vessels when they fell into a Swedish trap.

WHERE Svensksund, southern Finland.

WHEN July 8–10, 1790

WHY The Swedes had declared war on Russia to try to regain territories lost in Finland earlier in the century.

OUTCOME The Swedish were successful at Svensksund, but when the treaty to end the Russo-Swedish war was signed the following month it brought them no territorial gains.

Svensksund was the greatest naval defeat Russia had ever experienced by the time the battle took place and, even though it ended the Russo-Swedish War, it remains curiously uncelebrated in Sweden.

RUSSO-SWEDISH WAR

SWEDISH VICTORY

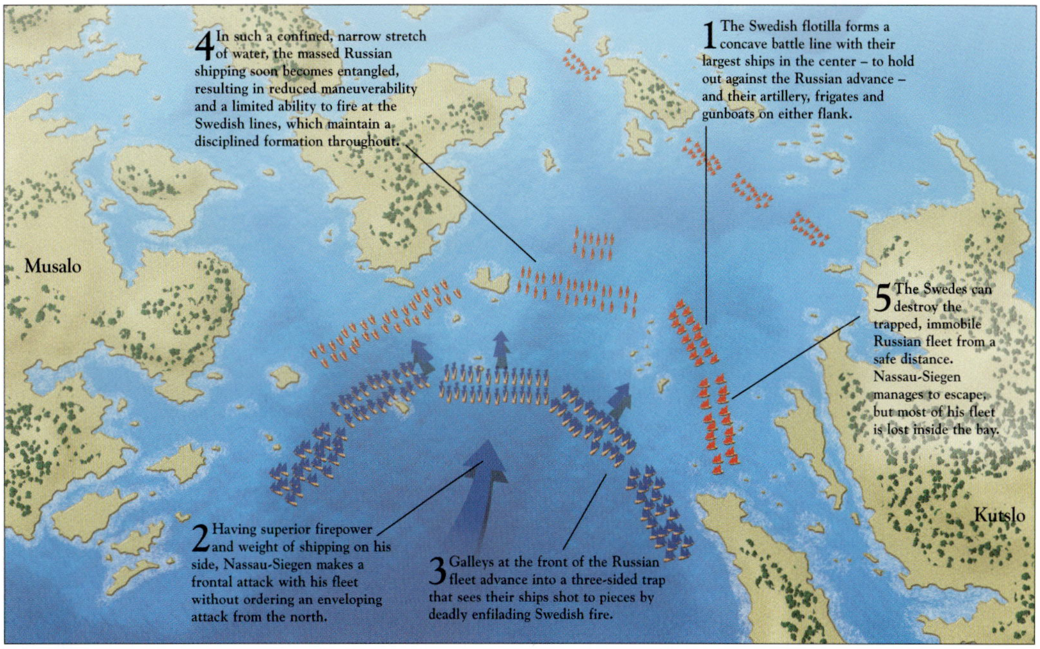

The Russians deployed a larger fleet at Svenskund, but made a huge mistake by opting for a purely frontal offensive. They sailed right into a Swedish trap, leaving them open to flanking fire on both sides, and negating their numerical advantage.

King Gustavus III of Sweden had been keen to provoke a fight with Russia, partly to regain land lost in Finland to the Russians 50 years earlier. But earlier battles hadn't gone well, and the first battle of Svensksund, in 1789, had been lost. The following year, however, King Gustavus, in personal command of a 250-strong flotilla, waited with his ships in a strong defensive position along the northern edge of the bay in anticipation of another Russian attack.

SWEDISH TRAP

Underestimating his enemy's strength and leadership, the Russian commander Charles von Nassau-Siegen signalled his 150 vessels to make a frontal assault. As his ships advanced, they sailed into the trap the Swedes had laid for them, coming under heavy enfilading fire from their flanks. In the confusion, the Russian vessels drifted ever deeper into the Swedish trap until they could no longer move or maneuver properly and were shot to pieces. Nassau-Siegen finally admitted defeat, but the signalled retreat could not be executed. The Russians lost 7400–9500 men and almost 90 vessels were either sunk or captured.

LOCATION

Svensksund, or "Swedish Sound," is situated in the eastern part of the Finnish archipelago, south of the towns of Kotka and Fredrikshamn (Hamina).

TIMELINE

1500–1000BC	1000–500BC	500BC–0AD	0–500AD	500–1000AD	1000–1500AD	1500–2000AD

Glorious First of June 1794

KEY FACTS

WHO	Admiral Lord Howe leads the British fleet against the French fleet led by Vice-Admiral Louis Thomas Villaret de Joyeuse, protecting a French grain convey.
WHAT	Admiral Lord Howe tried to divide the French line so the ships could be picked off individually, but his plan was misunderstood by his captains, and while the French ships sustained significant damage, the convoy got through.
WHERE	Atlantic Ocean.
WHEN	June 1, 1794
WHY	With famine looming in France, a convoy had been sent to secure supplies from its American colonies.
OUTCOME	Britain's naval superiority saw the French lose seven ships, yet the ultimately successful arrival of the convoy was treated as a victory by the French.

In 1794, the French, in the midst of a series of wars with its neighbors and with its ports under blockade, was facing serious food shortages. It had to turn to its colonies across the Atlantic for aid.

FRENCH REVOLUTIONARY WARS

NO CLEAR VICTORY

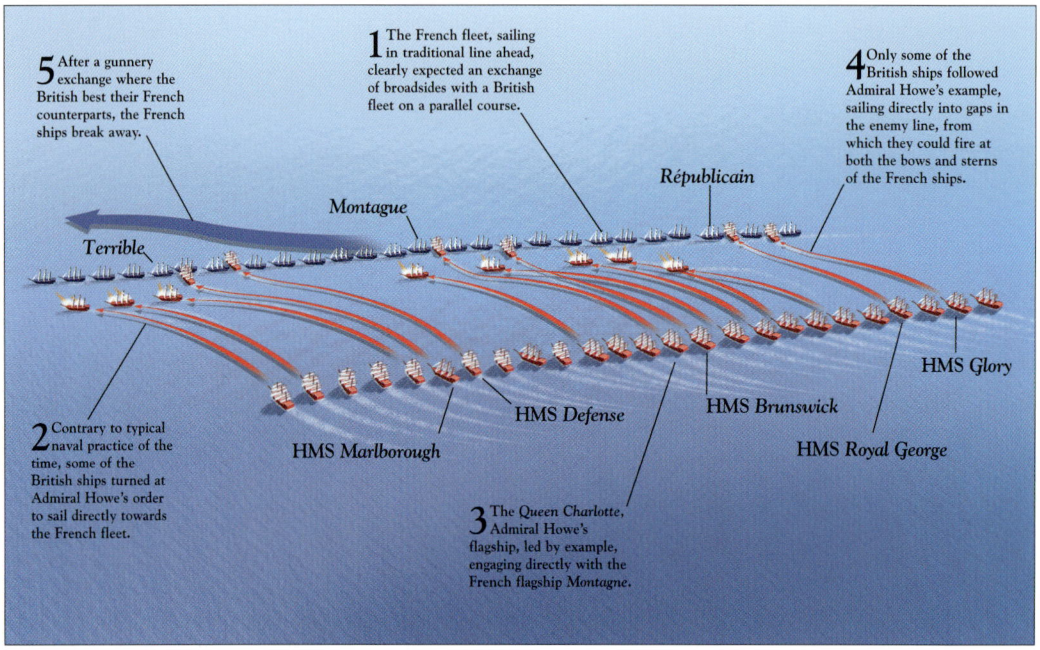

Admiral Lord Howe broke with the conventional pattern of a naval exchange of the time, which usually involved parallel lines of boats firing broadsides at each other, by sailing directly into the lines of his opponents.

LOCATION

Admiral Howe chased the French Brest fleet into the open Atlantic, where it had been ordered to protect a grain convoy from America.

As a French convoy, loaded with grain, made its return journey across the Atlantic, Admiral Lord Howe at the head of the British fleet made ready to intercept it, finally catching up with the French fleet that was escorting it home on June 1, a month after it had departed the shores of Virginia.

Howe boldly planned to send his ships to pierce the French line individually and break through to their leeward, cutting off the French line of retreat. This would allow him either to scatter or destroy the ships in a piecemeal fashion. However, he only partially succeeded—most of his captains misunderstood or ignored his signals.

Howe's flagship, *Queen Charlotte*, and five other British vessels pierced the French line in a ragged attack, saved from serious damage by poor French gunnery. The battle became a confused mêlée, as ships engaged in individual duels. After some fierce exchanges, the French finally broke away, leaving seven captured and sunk ships behind. However, the British fleet was too badly damaged to pursue. Only one of the actual cargo ships had been lost when the convoy finally reached Brest.

TIMELINE

1500–1000BC	1000–500BC	500BC–0AD	0–500AD	500–1000AD	1000–1500AD	1500–2000AD

Fleurus 1794

KEY FACTS

WHO General Jean-Baptiste Jourdan, general-in-chief of the French army, faced a large Austrian and Dutch relief force led by the Prince of Sachsen-Coburg.

WHAT Jourdan had laid siege to Charleroi, and managed to beat off an attempted relief force at nearby Fleurus.

WHERE Fleurus, Belgium.

WHEN June 26, 1794

WHY The French had occupied Belgium and Holland, but the Coalition armies had succeeded in driving them back to the French frontier.

OUTCOME Victory enabled the French to push on with their conquest of Belgium and, eventually, the Netherlands.

The Battle of Fleurus, which featured the first use of "airpower" in warfare—in the shape of an air balloon used by the French for reconnaissance—was a key battle in the French Revolutionary Wars. By winning it, the French paved the way for the ultimate break-up of the Dutch Republic.

FRENCH REVOLUTIONARY WARS

FRENCH VICTORY

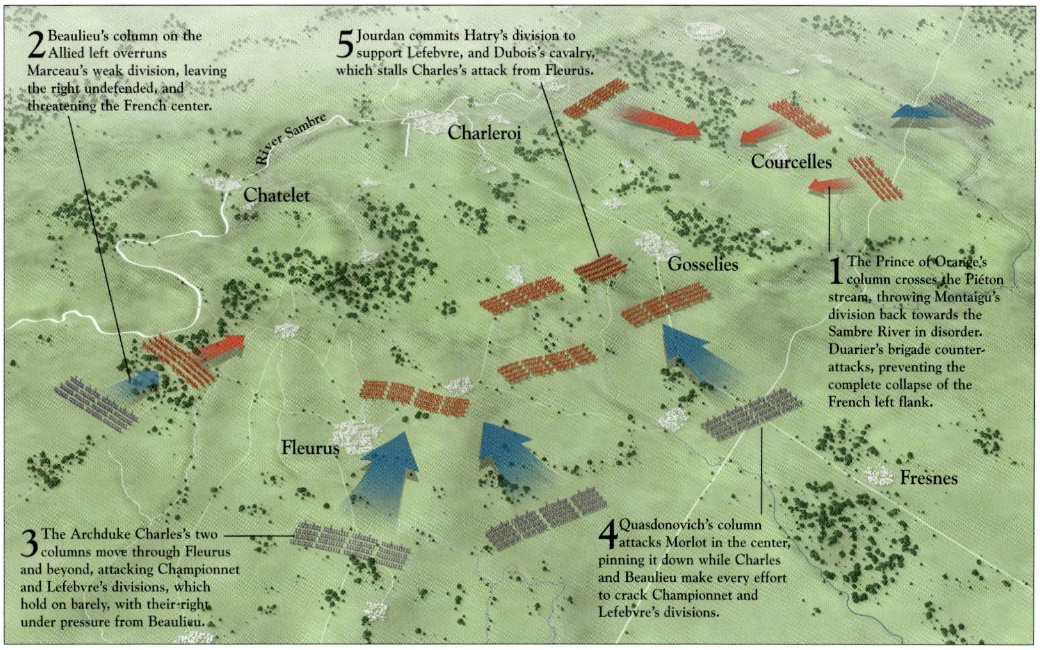

The occupation of the Low Countries by the French Revolutionary Army inevitably caused alarm in neighboring countries, and a coalition of various interests was formed, converging on the French near Fleurus.

LOCATION

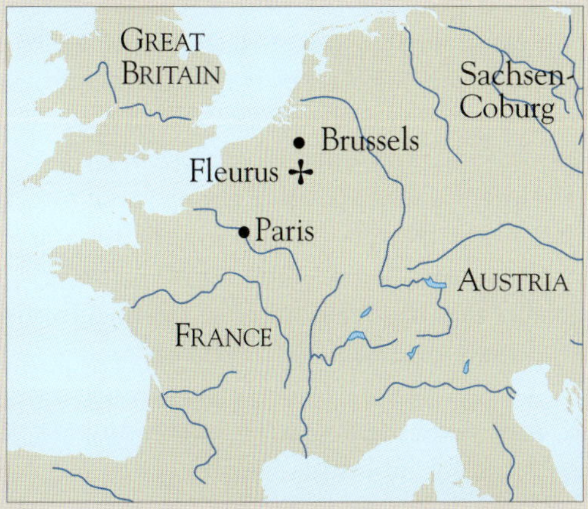

After several failed attempts to capture Charleroi, the French finally succeeded in June 1794, defeating the relief army under the Prince of Sachsen-Coburg.

The Austrian and Anglo–Allied armies successfully threatened the French occupation of Belgium and Holland in the spring of 1794, with a counteroffensive forcing them to withdraw their armies to the French frontiers. The Committee of Public Safety set up during the French Revolution dispatched the bloodthirsty deputy Louis de St. Just to ensure the armies and their commanders understood the severity of the situation.

SIEGE OF CHARLEROI

General Jean-Baptiste Jourdan, temporarily removed from command in 1793, was appointed general-in-chief of a new invasion force and crossed the Sambre river to besiege Charleroi. The Prince of Sachsen-Coburg headed an Austrian-Dutch attempt to relieve the city, but Jourdan deployed his army in a semicircle to prevent it reaching its destination, at Fleurus.

After a desperate battle in which Jourdan's flanks broke, his ability to deploy his reserves rapidly, combined with the steadfastness of his center, forced the allies to withdraw from the field with heavy casualties. The French were able to push on with their conquest.

TIMELINE

1500–1000BC	1000–500BC	500BC–0AD	0–500AD	500–1000AD	1000–1500AD	1500–2000AD

Rivoli 1797

FRENCH REVOLUTIONARY WARS

FRENCH VICTORY

KEY FACTS

Who Napoleon Bonaparte at the head of the French Army of Italy against Baron General Jozsef Alvinczy's Austrians.

What The Austrians, despite outnumbering the French, found themselves caught on unfavorable high ground above Rivoli, where their columns became disordered, and the greater experience of the French proved decisive on rough terrain.

Where Rivoli, Italy.

When January 14–15, 1797

Why Napoleon Bonaparte had laid siege to the city of Mantua, a key location for the Austrians as they attempted to fight back against the French onslaught in Italy.

Outcome After one of his greatest military victories, Bonaparte was able to further assert his hold on northern Italy.

Napoleon Bonaparte had invaded northern Italy in 1796, keen to sweep away the Austrians and set up a Republic. It was never going to be that easy, but at Rivoli he scored one of his most emphatic military victories.

Louis Albert Guislain Bacler d'Albe, French artist, cartographer, and adviser to Napoleon from 1796–1814, depicts here Napoleon and Masséna. Napoleon made Bacler d'Albe a Baron of the Empire and Masséna a Marshal of the Empire.

LOCATION

The Austrians under Alvinczy collected their forces to attack Napoleon's forces in Italy, thereby relieving one of their armies trapped in the fortress of Mantua.

Mantua was the last major town controlled by the Austrians, and its fortress had been besieged by Napoleon. Determined to lift the siege, the Austrians reinforced their army in northern Italy under Baron General Jozsef Alvinczy.

The plan was for Alvinczy's 28,000-strong force to come down the Adige valley from the north, forcing the narrow bottleneck in the mountains near Rivoli. When news reached Napoleon that the French under General Joubert had retreated to high ground at Rivoli, he ordered a division under General André Masséna at Verona to proceed there with all haste. When Napoleon himself arrived, he prepared for an immediate attack.

Alvinczy had divided his force into six separate assault columns. Three columns would attack the heights to which the French had retreated. Two other columns were to march along both banks of the Adige and attempt to scale the gorge on to the heights. A sixth column, under General Lusignon, was to undertake a flanking maneuver along the French right, coming in on the rear of Napoleon's army and cutting off their escape.

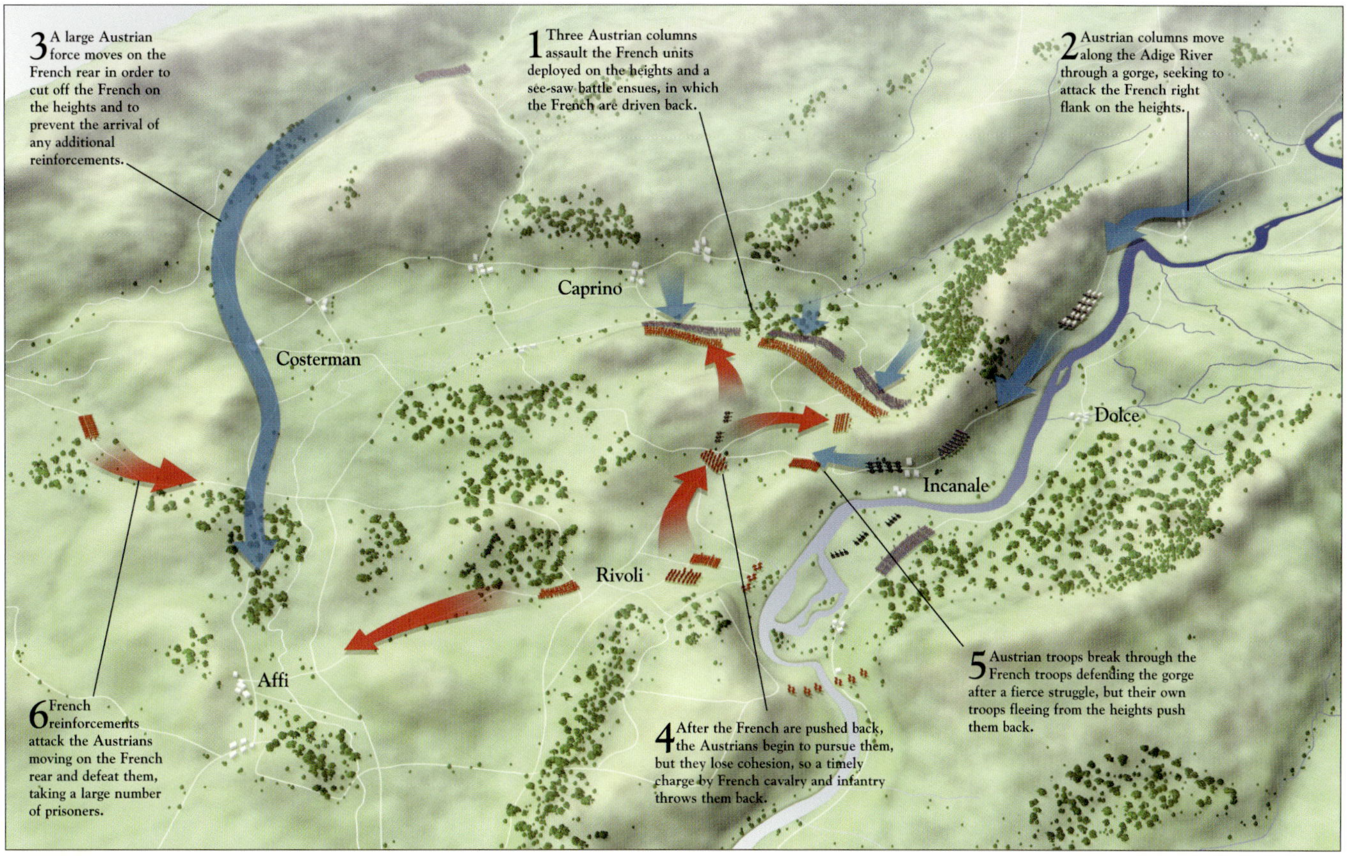

The Battle of Rivoli took place on tricky North Italian upland terrain. The deep, narrow gorges were especially perilous for the Austrians, many lacking the campaign experience of Napoleon's men.

The majority of Joubert's troops, including 18 artillery pieces, were on the heights, and they attacked the Austrians at first light. Despite being outnumbered by a factor of 4:3, the French attack went well at first, with the French capturing a key village from the Austrians.

But as the attack slowed, the Austrians were able to attack the exposed left on the French line, causing the unit of the 85th Demi-Brigade to flee. Only reinforcements brought by General Masséna were able to stabilize the now vulnerable left flank. Meanwhile, in the French center, a battalion of Austrian grenadiers overran a French battery in front of the 14th Demi-Brigade. Only a last-ditch bayonet charge enabled the French to recapture it.

The French right flank was also opened up when the 39th were forced from their defensive works. However, the difficult nature of the terrain slowed the advance of the Austrian forces, and a house provided with a large enclosure served as a rallying point for the units, soon to be augmented by reinforcements arrived from Lake Garda.

Things looked bleak for the French, and got worse. Volleys were heard from their rear—Lusignon's column had competed its flanking move, blocking not only the line of retreat but also the route the reinforcements would take. Responding to the dismay of some of his officers, Napoleon is reported to have said simply: "They are ours."

On the plateau, the French were able to sway the situation in their favor, as a small body of 200 cavalry attacked the Austrians troops. The Austrians were tired, and had lost much of their cohesion now that they were in pursuit. As a result, they were easily overthrown by this small body of cavalry. The panic that ensued, spread from one column to another, some even fleeing into the gorge, thereby pushing back the troops trying to ascend the heights. This allowed Joubert to lead a regiment to the edge of the gorge and fire on to the troops below, driving them back. Shortly thereafter, fresh French reinforcements arrived, trapping Lusignon's column between two enemy bodies. The tide had quickly turned in Napoleon's favor.

The battle had been won by the late afternoon, leaving Joubert merely to conduct a mopping up operation. Mantua fell the following month, and Napoleon continued his march through Italy.

TIMELINE

1500–1000BC	1000–500BC	500BC–0AD	0–500AD	500–1000AD	1000–1500AD	1500–2000AD

Rivoli

RIVOLI

The Austrian baron General Jozsef Alvinczy was, apparently, a keen admirer of the Prussian military mastermind Frederick the Great. He was keen to put his hero's ideas into operation with his own army. But Alvinczy was no Frederick, and his soldiers lacked experience. When he attempted to deploy a complicated formation at Rivoli, he came unstuck against one of the fighting greats of own time, Napoleon Bonaparte. Napoleon was a practical man as much as a thinker, able to react to fast-changing situations. He was at his peak in the mountain passes at Rivoli—as the more theoretical Alvinczy found to his cost.

Nile 1798

KEY FACTS

Who British forces led by Rear-Admiral Horatio Nelson, against the French Navy led by Vice-Admiral François Breuys.

What Nelson caught the French fleet in the bay at Aboukir unprepared for battle and partially unmanned. Most of the French ships were either sunk or taken by the British.

Where Aboukir Bay, Egypt.

When August 1, 1798

Why Napoleon had invaded Egypt, intending to continue on to British India, opening up new fronts in the war between the two nations. The ships that had delivered his army remained in Aboukir Bay.

Outcome The destruction of the French fleet undid the successful campaign waged on land in Egypt by Napoleon—and left him stranded. It also put the British Navy in control of the Mediterranean.

At the Battle of the Nile, Horatio Nelson dealt a body blow to the French fleet, caught napping in the Aboukir Bay. While the British fleet destroyed many of France's finest ships, it also left a certain Napoleon Bonaparte stranded in a foreign land.

FRENCH REVOLUTIONARY WARS

BRITISH VICTORY

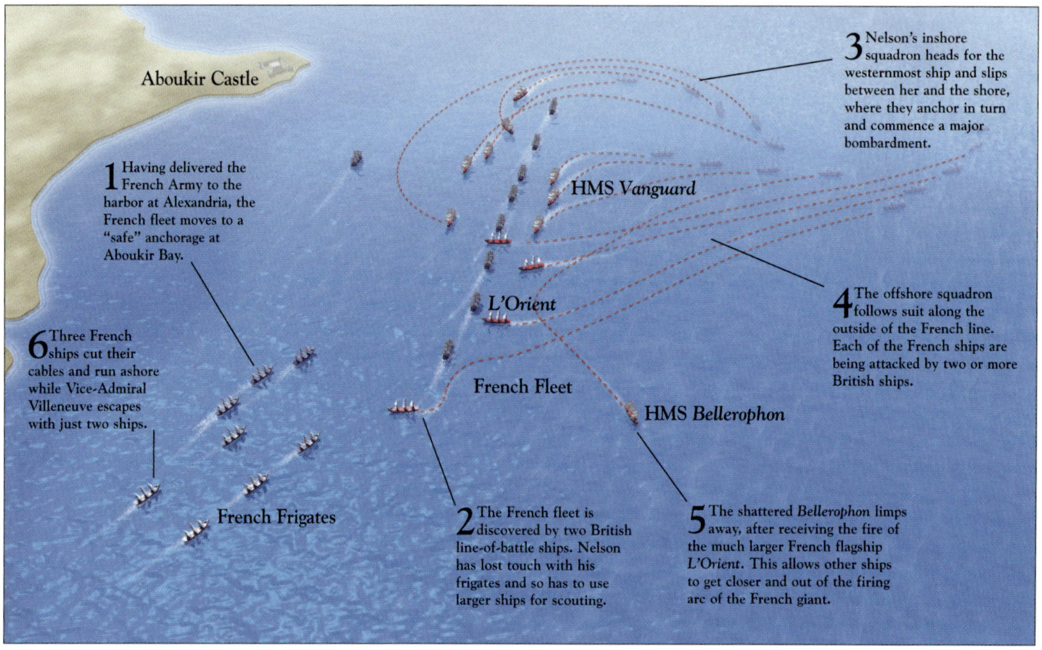

Nelson's deployment of his fleet at the Battle of the Nile meant that, although his force was technically outnumbered, there would be two of his ships for each one of the French.

After a French army, led by Napoleon, had disembarked on its Egyptian land campaign, the escorting fleet then anchored at Aboukir Bay. When Vice-Admiral Brueys learnt of the sudden approach of the British fleet, he chose to fight with his ships at anchor.

Admiral Nelson's battle plan involved splitting his ships into divisions, one to attack on the seaward side of the French, the other to cut in between where the fleet was anchored and the shoreline. It meant that the French would be caught in crossfire, and that even though, overall, Brueys had more ships and superiority in firepower, there would effectively be two British ships to every French one.

While the French center held for a time, gradually this told. When the flagship Orient suddenly exploded, Brueys was killed. His flag captain was also fatally wounded shortly afterwards.

With several French ships badly damaged, two others slipped out of line, then beached themselves, before surrendering. Just four French ships made good their escape. Nelson's victory also left the French army—and Napoleon—trapped in the Middle East.

LOCATION

Napoleon proved his detractors wrong and conquered Egypt, but he could not hold his gains because of lack of resupply from France.

TIMELINE

1500–1000BC	1000–500BC	500BC–0AD	0–500AD	500–1000AD	1000–1500AD	1500–2000AD

Copenhagen 1801

KEY FACTS

WHO Admiral Sir Hyde Parker and Vice-Admiral Lord Nelson led the British Navy against the fleet of Denmark-Norway

WHAT In a grimly fought battle, the exchanges grew so intense that Admiral Sir Hyde Parker actually directed a retreat signal at Nelson, who nonetheless persisted, enabling the superior gunnery of his ships eventually to come out on top.

WHERE Off-shore of Copenhagen, Denmark.

WHEN April 2, 1801

WHY British trade in the Baltic had been threatened by the formation of a League of Armed Neutrality, which the Scandinavian countries had joined.

OUTCOME An armistice was signed and Copenhagen re-opened to British trading ships.

The Battle of Copenhagen has gone down in history as the occasion when Lord Nelson, under orders to retreat, put his telescope to his blind eye and pretended not to see the signal. The result was one of his most hard-earned victories.

FRENCH REVOLUTIONARY WARS

BRITISH VICTORY

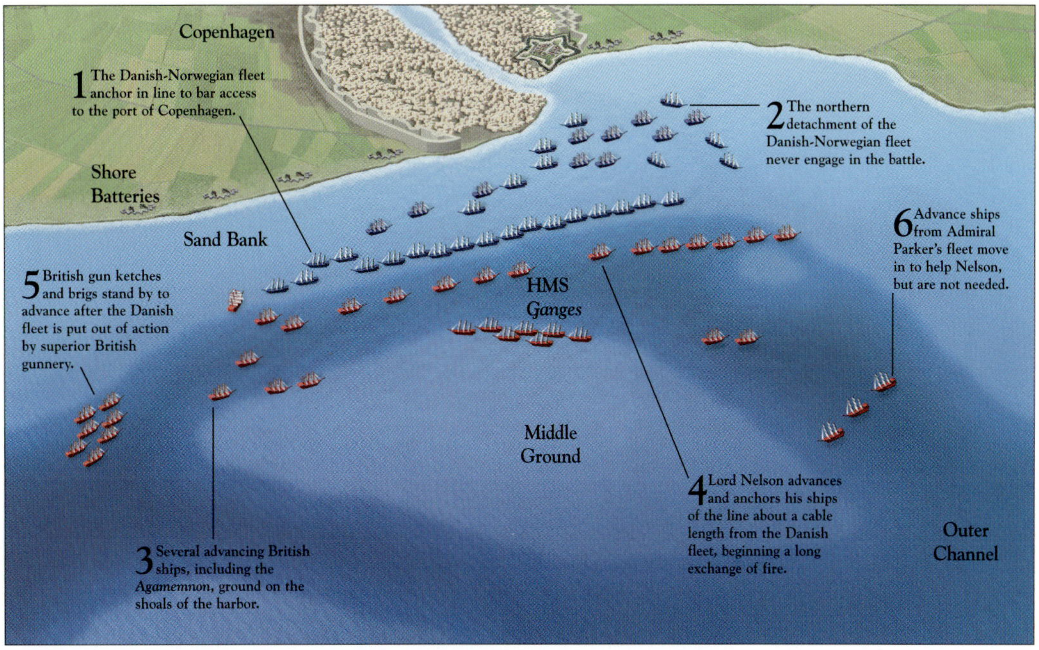

Copenhagen was a long, hard slog, with the two adversaries lining their ships alongside each other and pounding away with their guns. It was a battle that added to the legend of Nelson.

Admiral Sir Hyde Parker sent his second-in-command, Horatio Nelson, into Copenhagen harbor with 12 ships of the line that had relatively shallow draughts, along with the smaller vessels in the fleet. Consequently, three British ships grounded while entering the harbor, but the remaining vessels anchored about 200 yards (180m) from the Danish ships and batteries. From this position the two sides proceeded to fire broadsides at each other until each ship was disabled.

BREACH OF ORDERS

In light of the heavy Danish resistance, Parker signalled a retreat, which Nelson disregarded, famously putting his telescope to his blind eye and remarking to his captain: "I have only one eye. I have a right to be blind sometimes." Nelson was justified as superior gunnery disabled the Danish ships and British bomb vessels were able to approach the city. The battle ended when the Danes accepted an offer of truce.

Copenhagen is often considered to be Nelson's hardest fought battle, surpassing even the intensive fighting that took place at Trafalgar.

LOCATION

The Battle of Copenhagen was a result of failed diplomacy in Britain's attempt to break up the pro-French trading block of the League of Armed Neutrality.

TIMELINE

1500–1000BC	1000–500BC	500BC–0AD	0–500AD	500–1000AD	1000–1500AD	1500–2000AD

Trafalgar 1805

KEY FACTS

Who A Franco-Spanish fleet of 33 ships under Admiral Pierre Villeneuve (1763–1806), opposed by an English fleet of 27 ships under Vice-Admiral Horatio Nelson (1758–1805).

What Rather than a conventional engagement between lines of battle, the English made a risky attack that allowed them to gain local superiority over the enemy.

Where Off Cape Trafalgar near the Straits of Gibraltar.

When December 2, 1805

Why The English needed to cripple the Franco-Spanish fleet to protect England from invasion.

Outcome The Franco-Spanish fleet was decisively defeated.

The war between England and France was a clash between a great naval power versus a great land power. In the same year that Emperor Napoleon of France won his major land victory at Austerlitz, his chance to invade the British Isles was forever lost off the coast of Spain.

NAPOLEONIC WARS

BRITISH VICTORY

Trafalgar saw many ships crammed together and fighting at point-blank range. Whoever could keep up the highest rate of fire and cause the most significant damage would come off best.

LOCATION

Villeneuve's desire to gather up even more line-of-battle ships to lift the blockade at Brest allowed him to get caught by the aggressive British fleet.

If Napoleon's dream of invading and defeating Britain was ever to reach fruition, he knew he would also have to defeat its navy. Appointing Pierre Villeneuve to command his fleet, Napoleon planned for it to link up with Allied naval forces from Spain and clear the English Channel of British warships. This would enable a fleet of small boats to land Napoleon's "Army of England" in Britain.

When word arrived that the Combined Fleet was in Cadiz, preparations began to send a British fleet to engage it, led by Nelson, on HMS *Victory*. Nelson eventually caught up with Villeneuve's fleet off Cape Trafalgar, in the Straits of Gibraltar. The Combined Fleet seemed in some disorder as the British formed up into two columns with the intent of punching through the enemy line and achieving local superiority by "doubling up" on enemy ships. This maneuver was risky because it exposed the lead ships—including HMS *Victory*—to broadside fire. However, Nelson felt that the poorly trained enemy gunners could not inflict much damage, especially since a rising sea made gunnery difficult.

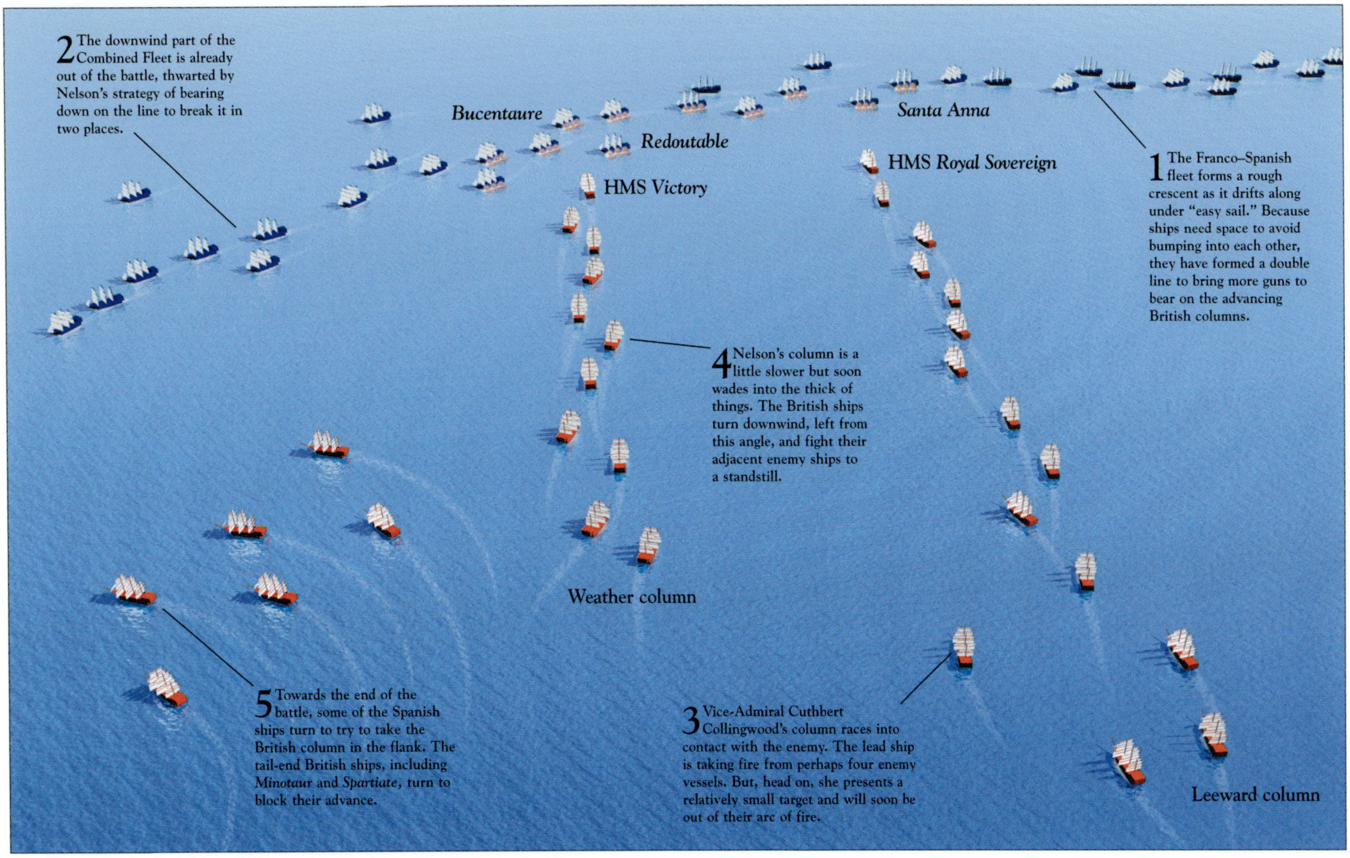

Breaking the enemy line, as Nelson did, was a risky approach but had a high payoff if the ships in the column managed to cut the line in two. As the British ships passed into the French line, they were able to deliver full broadside fire.

Within minutes of the first shots of the battle being fired, *Victory* was engaged with four enemy vessels. These included the most powerful warship in the world, the Spanish 136-gun first-rate *Santissima Trinidad* along with *Heros*, *Redoubtable* and the French flagship *Bucentaure*. Despite serious damage, *Victory* was able to pass under the stern of *Bucentaure*, allowing her entire broadside to fire down the length of the French flagship. With damage to her masts and steering, *Victory* was difficult to control and it was almost impossible to tell what was going on as a confused mêlée of ships began to develop. Nelson had refrained from making detailed plans with his captains, instead making them aware that they could do little wrong if they put their ship alongside one of the enemy and pounded it with guns.

Victory next engaged the *Redoubtable* and became entangled with her. Captain Jean-Jacques Lucas of the *Redoubtable* was aware of the limitations of his crew. Since gunnery and sailing training were problematic while under blockade, Lucas had drilled his crew in boarding actions and sharpshooting from the rigging.

Morale was high aboard *Redoubtable*, which carried a large force of marines. One of her sharpshooters hit Nelson, the bullet lodging in his spine. Nelson was taken below, where he died three hours later. In the meantime, Lucas and his crew were preparing to board *Victory*. Their attempt was disrupted when the second British ship in the line, the 98-gun *Temeraire*, fired into the crew assembled on *Redoubtable*'s deck.

Under fire from *Victory* and *Temeraire*, *Redoubtable* fought on until her crew had sustained almost 90 per cent casualties, most of them fatal. Then she finally struck her colors (indicating surrender), permitting *Victory* and *Temeraire* to double up on *Bucentaure*. Other ships fired into the French flagship as they passed, or joined the cannonade. *Santissima Trinidad* suffered the same treatment, refusing to surrender for hours despite not having any guns left to fight with.

By the time that a shattered *Bucentaure* surrendered to HMS *Conqueror*, the battle was ending. The French and Spanish had lost some 22 ships, the British none, though many vessels were severely damaged.

TIMELINE

1500–1000BC	1000–500BC	500BC–0AD	0–500AD	500–1000AD	1000–1500AD	1500–2000AD

Austerlitz 1805

KEY FACTS

WHO	73,000 French troops under Emperor Napoleon Bonaparte (1769–1821), opposed by an 85,000-strong Austro-Russian army commanded by Emperor Francis II (1768–1835) and Czar Alexander I (1777–1825).
WHAT	The Allies were drawn into an attack on the French left. Once committed on the flank, their center was broken by a French attack.
WHERE	Near Austerlitz in Bohemia, 60 miles (113 km) north of Vienna.
WHEN	December 2, 1805
WHY	The Allies feared that Napoleon intended to dominate Europe and moved to oppose him. The French responded with a brilliant campaign culminating in the victory at Austerlitz.
OUTCOME	The Allies were totally defeated, greatly weakening the Third Coalition that had formed to oppose Napoleon.

The war between England and France was a clash between a great naval power and a great land power. In the same year that Emperor Napoleon of France won his greatest land victory at Austerlitz, his chance to invade the British Isles was forever lost off the coast of Spain.

NAPOLEONIC WARS

FRENCH VICTORY

Austerlitz resulted in another victory for Napoleon Bonaparte, but with desperately high numbers of casualties suffered by both sides.

LOCATION

Outnumbered and deep in the heart of Moravia, Napoleon faced a Russo–Austrian Coalition army. His victory at Austerlitz was his greatest achievement.

When Napoleon, having decided that an invasion of Britain was impracticable, turned his full concentration on his mainland continental foes at the end of 1805 and occupied Vienna, the Austrian army chose not to fight and lose in a vain attempt to protect the capital. Instead, it moved off to prepare for a better opportunity for eventual victory. Napoleon, however, aware of the threat as long as his enemy's army remained in the field, determined to push on and seek a decisive action.

Reaching Brunn (Brno, now in the Czech Republic), he decided that he wanted to fight the Allies at a nearby location, next to the Pratzen Heights and the village of Austerlitz. To draw out the opposition, Napoleon posted forces on the Pratzen Heights and in Austerlitz, then hurriedly withdrew them as the enemy approached. To further consolidate the impression that he was in a bad position and wanted to avoid a battle, he entered into negotiations, and these were carried out with less of the arrogant self-confidence that characterized his usual manner.

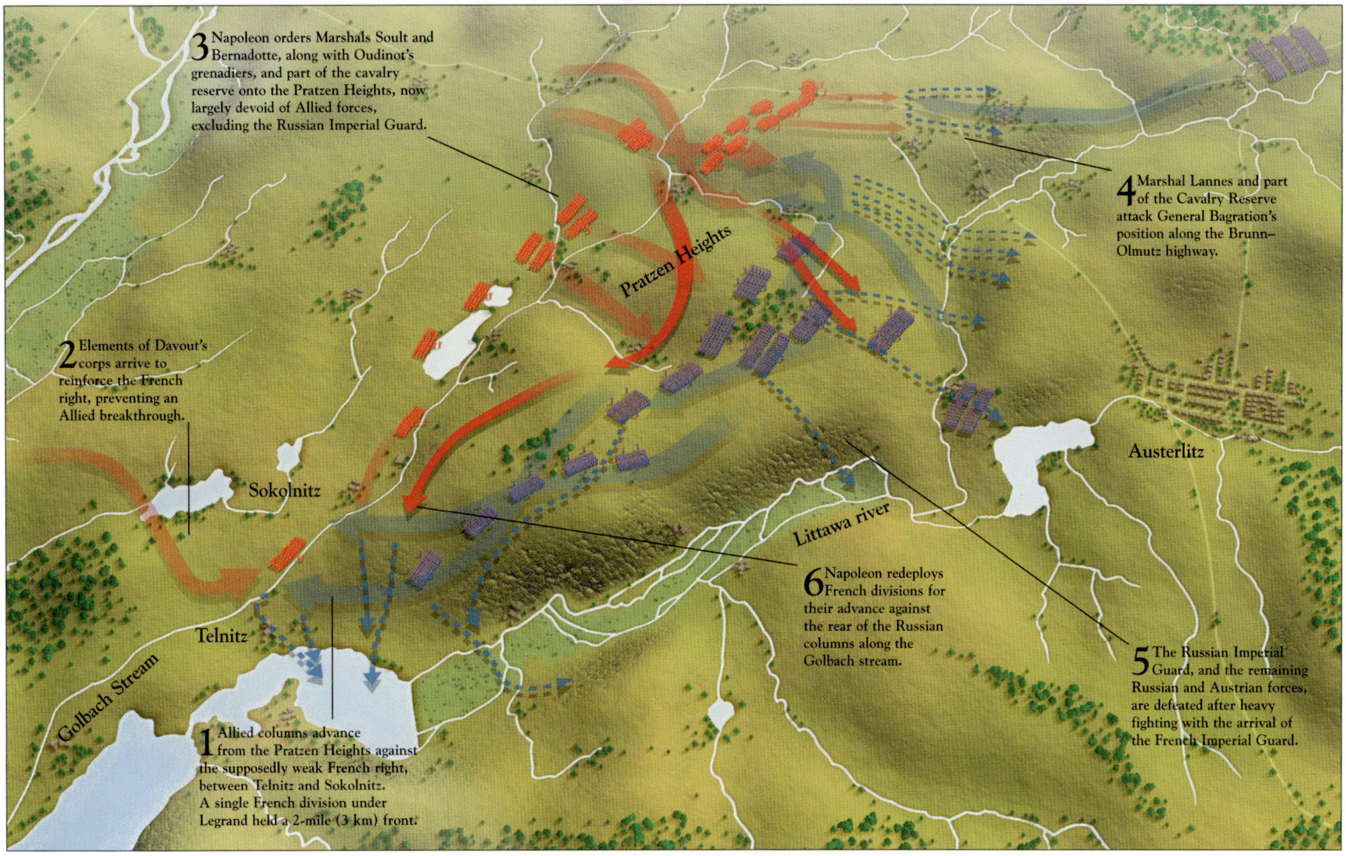

The raised ground of Pratzen Heights was the scene of most of the fighting during the Battle of Austerlitz. The battle showed the talents of Napoleon as a commander and tactician at their best, and his victory essentially destroyed the Third Coalition.

As most of their commanders were convinced that the French forces were weak and hesitant, the Allies decided to strike at the French right flank, which was understrength and in exposed positions. The intent was to break this flank while making a subsidiary attack on the opposite flank, opening the way for a final blow to rout the French army. This was exactly what Napoleon wanted them to try. They proceeded with their plan on the morning of December 2, 1805. The attack opened with an advance against the village of Tellnitz on the French right flank, but although there was a real danger for the French at this point that a determined Allied attack could drive in the flank as planned, the Allied advantage was not pressed home.

Napoleon waited until the Allies were fully committed to the attack on his right flank and had largely vacated the Pratzen Heights and then gave the order to attack. At the same time, he ordered a French corps to ascend the Heights, concealed in mist for at least some of the way, and take possession of them. A series of Russian counter-attacks failed to dislodge the French, who consolidated their position until they were in firm control of the center of the battlefield.

Czar Alexander also ordered his Imperial Guard to retake the Heights. Despite heavy resistance, they broke through the first French line and caused thousands of French soldiers to flee. As the French clung to the Heights, the Horse Grenadiers of the French Imperial Guard charged into action, beginning a mêlée that drew in large numbers of horsemen from both sides. This engagement was very closely fought, but the French, supported by horse artillery and steady infantry, gained the upper hand.

Now the Allies were weakening. Their flank attacks had failed and the surviving units were heavily engaged in close fighting, while the center was shattered. On the French right, the Allies finally broke and began to flee across the frozen lakes. The French artillery caused additional casualties by firing into the lakes to break the ice. However, there was little pursuit; the French, too, were exhausted by the heavy fighting. In addition to reducing Austria to military impotence, the legend of Napoleonic invincibility was greatly enhanced.

TIMELINE

1500–1000BC	1000–500BC	500BC–0AD	0–500AD	500–1000AD	1000–1500AD	1500–2000AD

Austerlitz

AUSTERLITZ
The Battle of Austerlitz took place on the high ground of Pratzen Heights, and was an example of Napoleon Bonaparte's brilliance in engineering a situation to ensure that a stand-off took place on terrain of his own choosing. His Austrian and Russian opponents were desperate to prevent him from marching on Vienna, and came up with a complicated plan to stop him, but Napoleon outmaneuverd them, including a feint to convey the impression that he considered himself to be in an unfavorable position, and catching them with a surprise attack as a concealing mist lay over the battlefield. This was one of the victories that made Napoleon's reputation.

Auerstädt 1806

KEY FACTS

Who A corps of the French army under Marshal Louis Davout against Prussians led by the Duke of Brunswick.

What Napoleon had sent corps to attack the rear of the Prussian army, but they found themselves under attack from a greater concentration of enemy forces at Auerstädt.

Where Auerstädt, Germany.

When October 14, 1806

Why Napoleon had launched an attack into Saxony in response to the signing of a new alliance between Prussia and Russia.

Outcome Napoleon was able to march on to further victories in Prussia, paving the way for an all-out assault on Russia.

The French army by the early 1800s was a highly efficient fighting machine. But as events at Auerstädt proved, scouting methods of the period still left much room for improvement.

NAPOLEONIC WARS

FRENCH VICTORY

Napoleon's army was never more ruthless than at Auerstädt. After defeating the Prussians, they pursued their beaten remnants for four hours after they'd fled the field.

LOCATION

At Auerstädt, one of Napoleon's corps d' armée was able not only to stand on its own against a superior force but defeat it.

In the summer of 1806, after the Prussians had formed an alliance with Russia, Napoleon crossed the borders of Saxony at the head of the French army. He had every reason to be confident in the manpower at his disposal. La Grande Armée used a flexible organizational structure, within which units could be transferred between formations at need. The basic unit was the corps, into which the French army had been divided since 1800. Each corps was a self-contained all-arms force of infantry, artillery and cavalry, capable of dealing with many opponents unsupported and defending itself until assistance arrived if it encountered a superior force.

By contrast, the Prussian army was "a walking museum piece," scarcely changed since the days of Frederick the Great. Its poor command structure meant many positions were held by more than one officer.

Napoleon reached Jena, where he prepared to meet the Prussian army. To crush his enemies more completely, he ordered the III corps under Marshal Louis Davout and the I corps under Jean Bernadotte to move to the east of the

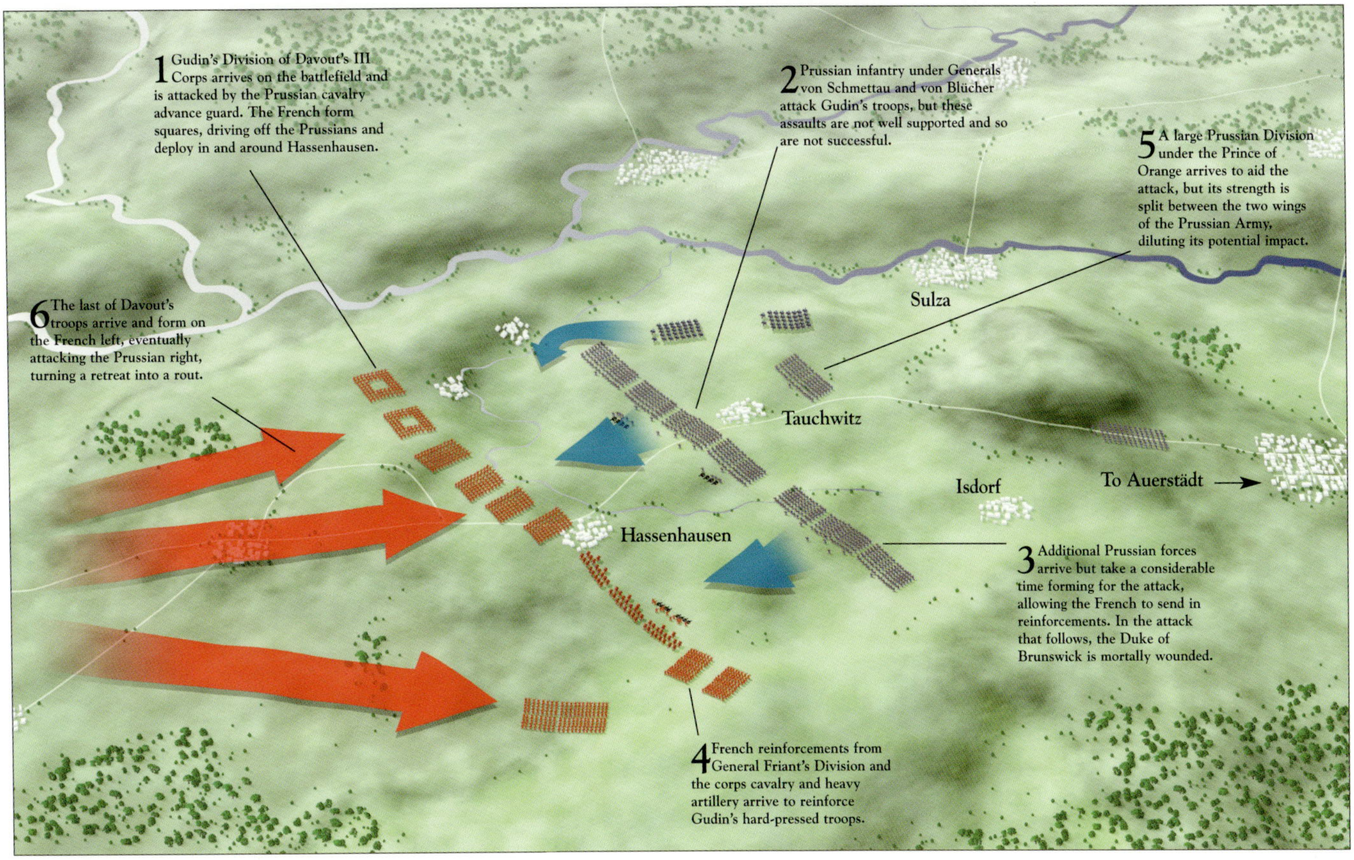

The Prussian army was a shadow of its former days under Frederick the Great when it took to the field at Auerstädt. Worse still, it was facing a highly efficient French army at the peak of its power and confidence.

town and make for the rear of the Prince of Hohenlohe's forces, cutting off their line of retreat.

FACE TO FACE

Davout's progress was slow since there was heavy fog and the terrain was a difficult climb. Worse still, and unknown to Napoleon, just about to do battle with what he had mistakenly been informed was the entire Prussian army on the heights above Jena, Davout's march was to bring him face to face with the main army, under the Duke of Brunswick, based at Auerstädt.

Almost immediately, Davout found himself under attack from an impetuous charge of two squadrons of Prussian dragoons. Ordering one brigade to form square, this was easily repulsed and, as the fog lifted, a horse battery under the command of General Etienne Gudin knocked out a Prussian battery and drove back some of their horse and foot. Davout then ordered Gudin to occupy the village of Hassenhausen, supported by the divisional artillery, where they drove back several uncoordinated attacks by Prussian infantry and cavalry.

Among these included one led by Gebhard Von Blücher who, impetuous as ever, had his horse shot out from under him, though he was able to return to his lines unharmed. At this critical moment French reinforcements arrived, just as William, the Prince of Orange, arrived with his division. Unfortunately, rather than keeping the division together and bringing its mass to bear on one of the flanks of the French Army, he was ordered to divide his command between the two flanks of the Prussian Army, thereby denying the opportunity to apply mass at a decisive point.

RELENTLESS PURSUIT

Further repeated Prussian charges were driven back. This, combined with the advance of fresh enemy troops, took the fight out of the Prussian infantry, which began to retire. By noon, the French were in a position to make a general advance, turning the retreat into a rout. The French were relentless and kept up the pressure on the retreating Prussians for nearly four hours, covering several miles before they halted, utterly exhausted.

TIMELINE

1500–1000BC	1000–500BC	500BC–0AD	0–500AD	500–1000AD	1000–1500AD	1500–2000AD

Maida 1806

KEY FACTS

WHO	General Sir John Stuart in charge of the British army against French troops commanded by General Jean Reynier.
WHAT	General Sir John Stuart was able to position his troops advantageously, so that they were able to inflict heavy losses on the advancing French lines while sustaining few himself.
WHERE	Maida, Calabria, Italy.
WHEN	July 4, 1806
WHY	The French were intending to invade Sicily, always a crucial island for its strategic position for trade, and the British were waging a campaign against them on the southern Italian peninsula.
OUTCOME	The British, by stoking up local opposition to the French, were able to stave off an invasion of Sicily.

In 1806, the southern peninsula of Italy was in turmoil, after the French invasion of Naples had forced its king to flee. Was there anything that stood in the way of them taking Sicily?

NAPOLEONIC WARS

BRITISH VICTORY

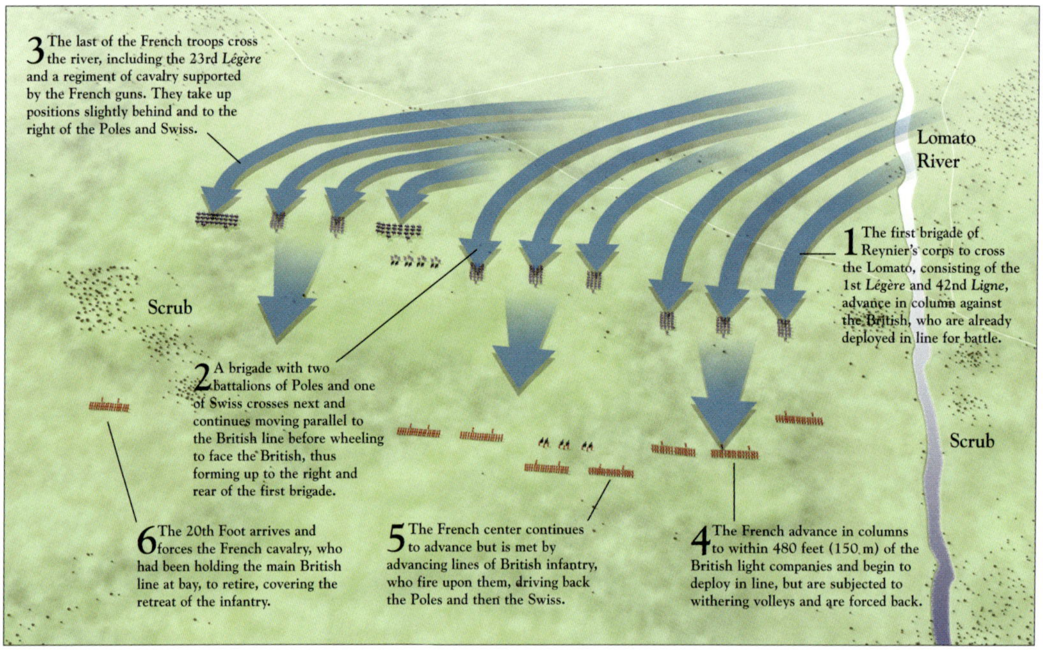

Maida lay on the tip of Naples and near the island of Sicily, for centuries an island whose considerable strategic significance, by virtue of its location, far outweighed its actual size.

LOCATION

The Battle of Maida was fought when the British landed a small army that drew French troops away from Gaeta, where Britain's allies were besieged.

General Sir John Stuart had landed a force of some 5000 infantry, supported by a battery of foot artillery, in Calabria in southern Italy with the dual intention of stirring local unrest against French occupation, and engaging the French in battle.

A French force under General Reynier met Stuart's army on a plain north of the Lomato River near the village of Maida. Since the French were south of the river, they had to march perpendicular to the British line of advance. While Stuart's troops formed for battle, the French crossed the Lomato and then wheeled to advance on the British. This forced Reynier's units to advance in an oblique battle order and did not allow them to deploy from column into line.

DEVASTATING VOLLEYS

The British units waited until the leading French columns were in range and unleashed devastating volleys. Most of the French infantry were forced to fall back, covered by cavalry who managed to prevent the British from fully exploiting what was already a sizeable tactical victory.

TIMELINE

1500–1000BC	1000–500BC	500BC–0AD	0–500AD	500–1000AD	1000–1500AD	1500–2000AD

Eylau 1807

KEY FACTS

Who General Levin von Bennigsen leading a Russian army against the French led by Napoleon Bonaparte.

What A gruelling battle in the snow, in which the French sustained heavy losses from Russian cannon, while the French retorted with a bloody cavalry charge. The Russians eventually retreated, but the French were too exhausted to pursue.

Where Preussische-Eylau, near Kalingrad.

When February 7–8, 1807

Why After routing the Prussians, Napoleon was now ready to carry his campaign into Russia.

Outcome The two sides slogged away for 14 hours and, with heavy casualties on both sides, no clear winner emerged. Napoleon would have to wait until the summer for the victory that would force the Russians to seek peace terms.

Fighting a battle in winter is generally inadvisable, and never was there a better illustration than at Eylau. Many who weren't killed suffered a perhaps worse fate by freezing to death while lying injured.

NAPOLEONIC WARS

STALEMATE

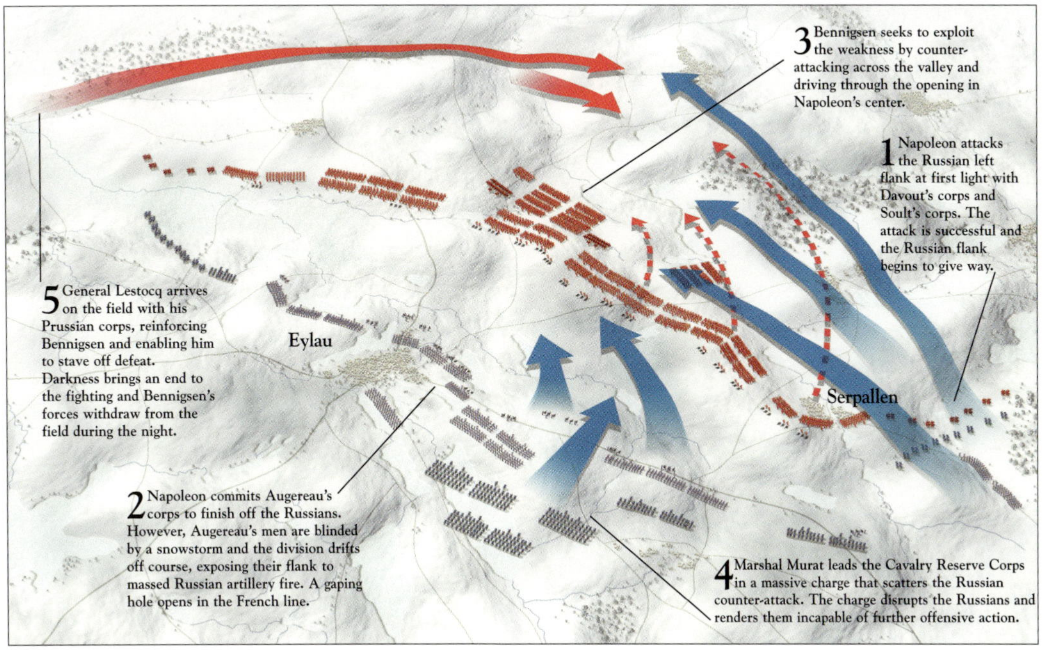

Some of the most punishing battles in history have been fought on Russian soil. Eylau took place in a snowstorm, and many combatants wounded in the exchanges simply froze to death.

Snow was falling when Napoleon launched a full-scale attack on General Levin von Bennigsen's lines at Eylau. Marshal Louis Davout conducted a brilliant attack that threatened to envelop the left flank of the Russian Army, but a supporting corps stumbled blindly through a snowstorm, lost its way and wandered directly into the path of the Russian main gun line. Torn to pieces by grapeshot, the corps fled from the field, leaving a gaping hole in Napoleon's line.

The Russians would have prevailed had not Marshal Joachim Murat launched a massive attack with the French Cavalry Reserve, which checked the Russian advance and saved the day. Bennigsen was reinforced by General Lestocq's Prussian corps late in the battle, and with these fresh troops he was able to stabilize his position, before staging a full retreat. The French were so exhausted they could not pursue them, having lost perhaps 25,000 men, to the Russians' and Prussians' 15,000. Many of the wounded froze to death. Marshal Ney, who had arrived late in the battle, tellingly surveyed the scene and commented: "What a massacre! And without a result!"

LOCATION

During a rare winter campaign, Napoleon attempted to destroy his Russian opponent in a major battle at the village of Eylau, in Russian Poland.

TIMELINE

1500–1000BC	1000–500BC	500BC–0AD	0–500AD	500–1000AD	1000–1500AD	1500–2000AD

Maida

MAIDA

Italy, in the years before its unification in the mid-nineteenth century, was perpetually caught up in the machinations of the colonial powers of Europe, with the Austrians and the Spanish Bourbons among those who took a hand in controlling its affairs. By the beginning of the nineteenth century, it was the French under Napoleon who seemed set to take control of the entire peninsula. This was a disaster for a trading nation like Britain, which needed access to the Mediterranean. Maida was fought in a plain near the Lomato River by a British army under General Stuart and thwarted French plans to invade strategically vital Sicily.

Friedland 1807

NAPOLEONIC WARS

FRENCH VICTORY

The battle of Friedland was notable as the moment when artillery truly came of age as a combat arm that was the equal of the cavalry and the infantry, a truly independent element of maneuver on the battlefield. It was a major moment on the road to modern warfare.

KEY FACTS

Who The Russian army under General Levin von Bennigsen against la Grande Armée of Napoleon.

What The French deployed close-range, rapid artillery fire to open the way for a decisive victory.

Where Friedland, modern day Pravdinsk, Russia.

When June 14, 1807

Why Napoleon had launched a major invasion of Russia, having previously defeated their Prussian allies.

Outcome Russia quickly sought terms with Napoleon, but peace would be short-lived.

Light cavalry, usually used for pre-battle reconnaissance and pursuit after enemy lines had been broken, played a full part in the mounted charges at Friedland.

LOCATION

Friedland brought to a conclusive end the campaigns that started in September 1806. Napoleon was now master of central Europe.

The Russian army under General Bennigsen was crossing the River Alle at Friedland when a French army marching under the command of Marshal Jean Lannes was sighted on the western bank of the river overlooking the town. Lannes apparently being unsupported, Bennigsen decided to cross the river and destroy his force. By deciding on this course of action, Bennigsen committed himself to fight with a river at his back.

Further, he had his pontonniers construct three bridges leading into Friedland and nowhere else, though he also had the civilian bridge over the river at his disposal. This plan of action limited Bennigsen's ability to withdraw quickly if necessary. Lannes immediately sent couriers galloping off to find Napoleon and the main French Army and proceeded to fight an expert delaying action against the Russians.

The French general never had more than 26,000 men at his disposal to face 60,000 Russians. Not only did Bennigsen fail to destroy Lannes' corps, he deployed almost his entire force against it, so when Napoleon

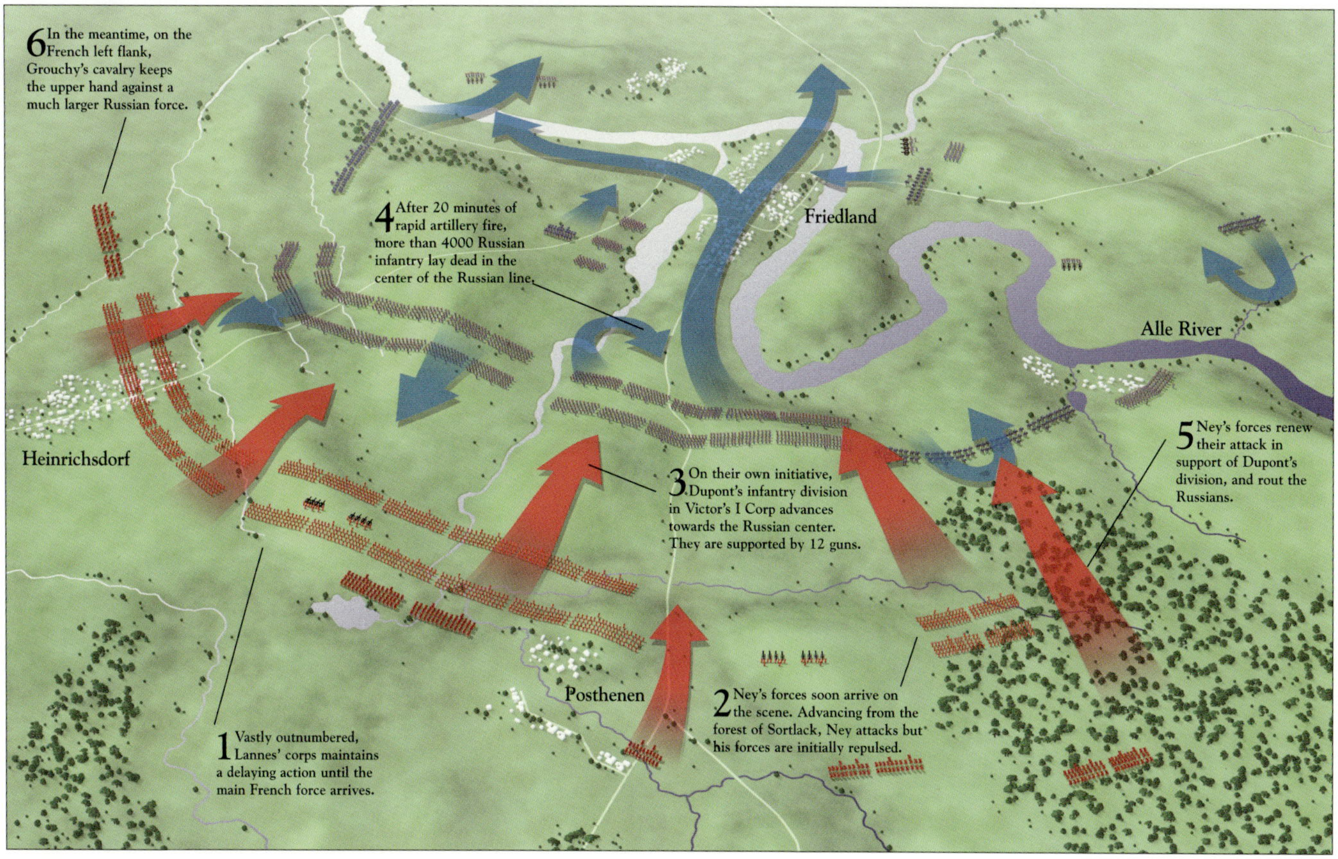

While the cavalry charge played a big role at Friedland, this was the first time artillery was used as an independent element of attack on the battlefield. Horse-drawn mobile artillery enabled commanders to concentrate fire at key moments and points in a battle.

finally arrived, he was presented with a golden opportunity to capitalize.

In the French center, General Sénarmont, the corps chief of artillery in I Corps, successfully requested the use of the entire corps artillery contingent, 36 guns, to join in an advance by General Pierre Dupont. Sénarmont initially formed the artillery into two 15-gun batteries on the flanks of Dupont's division. The other six guns were kept in reserve along with the ammunition caissons. The artillery batteries soon outpaced Dupont, and Sénarmont took the responsibility of ordering them forward against the Russian center. They advanced by bounds, opening fire on the Russians at approximately 450 yards (410 m) from the center of the enemy line. The Russian infantry stood firm. After firing five or six salvoes, Sénarmont ordered his companies forward, stopping at a range of 250 yards (230 m) to open fire once again.

Ordering his guns to cease firing, Sénarmont again ordered the companies forward, stopping once again to open fire, this time at 150 yards (135 m) from the Russian positions. Just over 20 minutes later, more than 4000 Russians littered the field and the Russian center was destroyed. This was the decisive action of the battle.

An attack by Marshal Ney followed up Sénarmont's maneuver. Dupont had also brought his division forward in support and defeated the Russian Guard infantry in close combat. Sénarmont was counter-attacked by the cavalry of the Russian Guard, and his artillery companies changed front and gave the Russian horsemen two canister volleys, shattering their charge.

ARTILLERY MANEUVER

The remainder of the battle was almost anticlimactic. The Russian left was crushed and there was a rush for the bridges. Ney and Dupont continued to advance and now Sénarmont supported the French advance on Friedland, their combined efforts nearly destroying the Russian Army. Friedland was one of the outstanding victories of the French Empire and its artillery tactics, repeated on other battlefields, marked the first time artillery had been used as an independent maneuver element on the battlefield in an offensive role.

Somosierra 1808

NAPOLEONIC WARS

FRENCH VICTORY

KEY FACTS

WHO Napoleon Bonaparte and the French Army, with the assistance of the Polish cavalry, against Benito San Juan leading a makeshift Spanish army, including conscripts and reservists.

WHAT Napoleon's advance on Madrid occurred when a mountain pass was blocked by Benito San Juan's army. A charge by the Polish cavalry was crucial to the French bursting through and continuing on to the capital.

WHERE The mountain pass near Somosierra, north of Madrid.

WHEN November 30, 1808

WHY Napoleon Bonaparte had launched an invasion of Spain, but despite the efficiency of the French army, there was much local resistance.

OUTCOME Napoleon was able to march on to Madrid, which fell to him a week later.

Spain had assisted Napoleon in his conquest of Portugal, but then found itself the object of his imperial attentions. The capital Madrid had risen up against him earlier in 1808, however, and now he found himself having to march on the city to stamp his control.

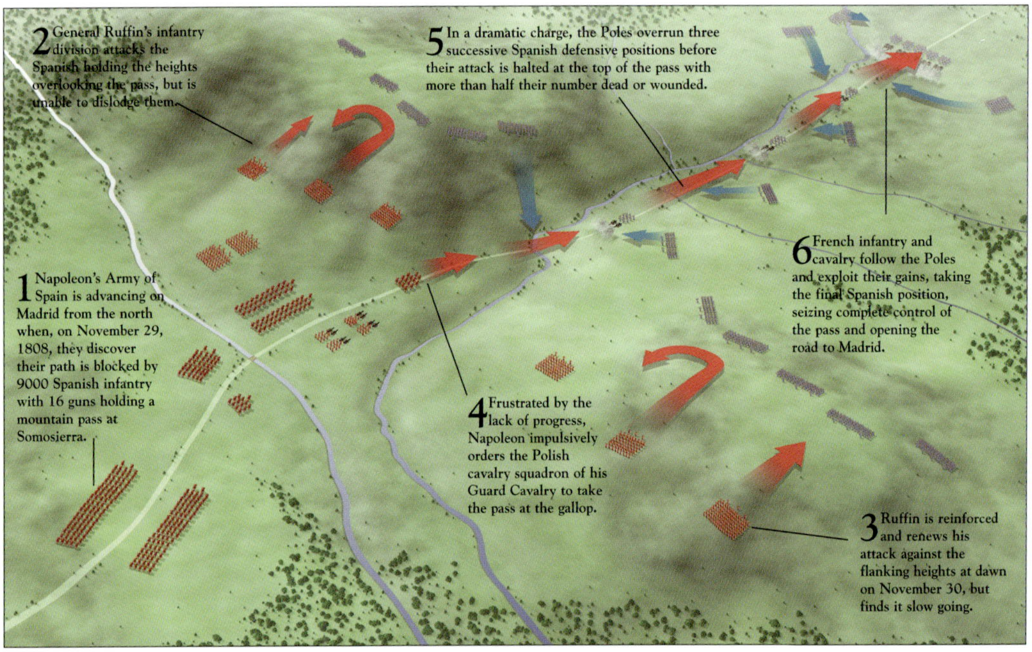

Even if the golden age of the cavalry was passing, mounted troops could still play a key part in warfare. At Somosierra, much was owed to the exploits of the Polish cavalrymen who took the mountain pass at a gallop.

LOCATION

The village of Somosierra is located at the top of a strategic mountain pass along one of the main roads leading to the Spanish capital of Madrid.

Napoleon's 40,000-strong Army of Spain was driving towards the capital Madrid. But Benito San Juan had managed to put together a respectably sized force, based around local militia, reservists and conscripts. And with 16 guns ensconced in fortified positions astride a mountain pass winding past the town of Somosierra, he had blocked the route.

CLEARING THE WAY

General Francois Ruffin's infantry division attempted but failed to clear the Spanish from the heights overlooking the pass, but progress was slow. As Napoleon fumed at the delay, one of the advance Spanish batteries fired on his headquarters. At his order, his Polish escort squadron of 125 troopers charged forward and overran the first gun battery, then pressed on, capturing two more gun positions and practically clearing the road all the way to the summit before heavy casualties brought them to a halt. French infantry and cavalry then rushed forward and captured the final Spanish position at Somosierra, thus opening up the road to Madrid, which Napoleon captured shortly afterwards.

TIMELINE

1500–1000BC	1000–500BC	500BC–0AD	0–500AD	500–1000AD	1000–1500AD	1500–2000AD

Wagram 1809

NAPOLEONIC WARS

FRENCH VICTORY

KEY FACTS

Who	Napoleon Bonaparte and the French Army, against the Austrians, led by Archduke Charles of Austria.
What	In a punishing battle, marked by extensive use of artillery, Napoleon was able to gain a morale-boosting win after recent setbacks.
Where	Deutsch-Wagram, near Vienna, Austria.
When	July 5–6, 1809
Why	The Austrians, believing Napoleon would be preoccupied by the Peninsular War, had launched a fightback.
Outcome	The French actually suffered huge losses in the battle, as did the Austrians, leading to the signing of a peace treaty framed much in Napoleon's favor.

Napoleon Bonaparte had just suffered his first major defeat on the battlefield when he leapt back into action a few weeks later. Victory at Wagram somewhat restored his tarnished lustre, but at a huge cost in human life. For the second time, his army suffered immense caualties.

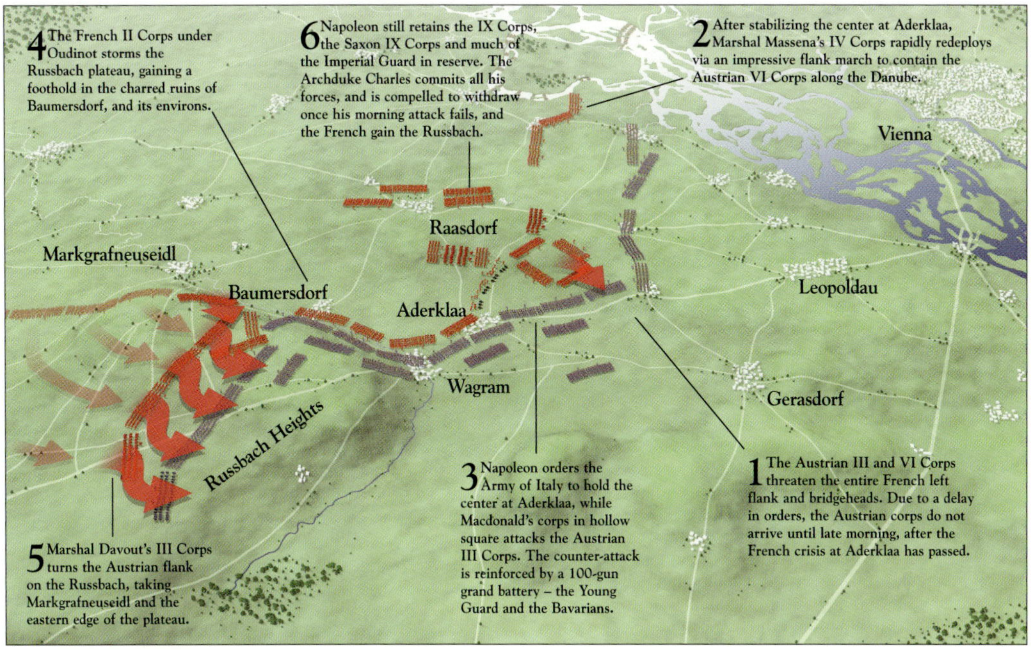

The French success at Wagram owed much to a nighttime river maneuver that bore more similarities to a modern special forces operation than a conventional battle.

Little more than month after a heavy defeat by the Austrians at Aspern-Essling, on the Danube near Vienna, Napoleon decided to return to the battlefield, determined not to repeat the mistakes that had led to that defeat. This time, the French Army constructed gun emplacements, deployed heavy batteries and built numerous pontoon bridges for a second crossing of the Danube. They then managed a remarkably swift and efficient night-time crossing, which resembled an early nineteenth-century special forces operation rather than a conventional battle. The Austrian divisions guarding the bank were overwhelmed, and within four hours Napoleon had three full corps across the river. A violent battle characterized by extensive artillery bombardment ensued, during which the French would lose 30,000 men (it had lost as many at Aspern-Essling). The Austrians, however, fared even worse.

After Wagram, Austria was unable to summon the will to continue the hostilities, and agreed to an armistice. The terms of the peace treaty were shaped more to Napoleon's liking than to his opponent's.

LOCATION

Archduke Charles met Napoleon for a second time on the north bank of the Danube, across from French-occupied Vienna.

TIMELINE

1500–1000BC	1000–500BC	500BC–0AD	0–500AD	500–1000AD	1000–1500AD	1500–2000AD

Wagram

WAGRAM

Napoleon Bonaparte was nothing if not the nineteenth-century comeback kid of both the political and military arenas. He fought Wagram just weeks after a bad shaking at the hands of the Austrians at Aspern-Essling, but this time he was triumphant. However, victory at Wagram, achieved with much use of artillery bombardment ensued, came at a heavy price. The French would lose 30,000 men, following on from similarly heavy casualties in the earlier battle. That said, the Austrians lost even more soldiers, and it was Napoleonic France that emerged distinctly the stronger from the resultant armistice.

Grand Port 1810

KEY FACTS

Who Captain James Willoughby of the HMS *Nereide*, against a small squadron of the French navy under Captain Guy-Victor Duperre.

What Captain Willoughby attempted to lure French ships into a trap at Grand Port, Ile de France, but the plan backfired and ultimately led to much loss of life.

Where Off Grand Port, Ile de France, Mauritius.

When August 1810

Why The British and French navies were battling to attain supremacy in the Indian Ocean, with French corsairs attacking British trade ships.

Outcome After this embarrassing British naval defeat, Willoughby was blamed for giving misleading information about the extent of the threat posed by the French force.

During the Napoleonic period, the British and French fleets battled furiously for control of the Indian Ocean. Generally, the British had the stronger presence, but they endured a substantial setback in 1810.

NAPOLEONIC WARS

FRENCH VICTORY

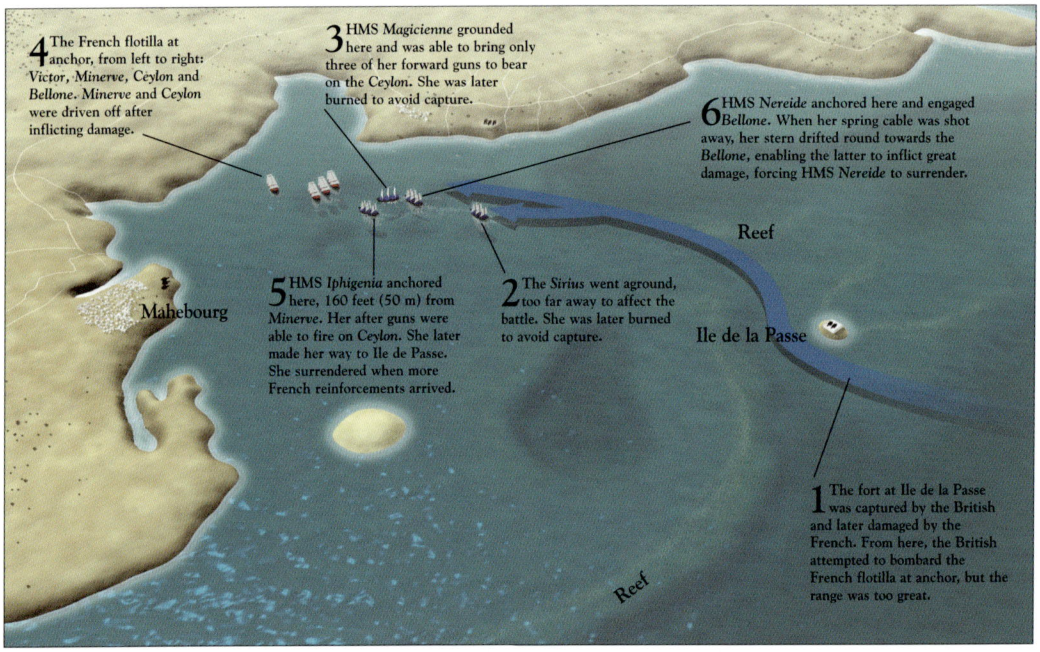

The defeat of the British fleet in this confrontation in the Indian Ocean would be one of the biggest setbacks the Royal Navy suffered during the Napoleonic Wars.

The British sought to respond to French harassment of its ships sailing to and from its Indian colonies by blockading Grand Port on the French held Ile de France. Captain James Willoughby of the HMS *Nereide*, the senior British officer and an old India hand, had been dispatched to capture a battery on the island, but spotted the approach of five French frigates.

CUNNING TACTICS

Realizing the French were unaware of his presence, he sought to lure them into the harbor by raising the French tricolor. As the first ship, a small corvette, came close, Willoughby opened fire and sent small boats to capture the ship. They could not reach it, however, and the other French ships, by now wise to Willoughby's ruse, returned fire—one caused an explosion on the island, killing several of Willoughby's men. With many others of his crew in small boats offshore, the opportunity to cause significant damage to the French ships had been lost.

Subsequently the French were able to inflict great damage on the remainder of the British squadron, leading to its worst naval defeat in the Napoleonic Wars.

LOCATION

The French naval threat in the Indian Ocean had to be met by the Royal Navy to safeguard merchant shipping from India and the Far East.

TIMELINE

1500–1000BC	1000–500BC	500BC–0AD	0–500AD	500–1000AD	1000–1500AD	1500–2000AD

Siege of Badajoz 1812

KEY FACTS

WHO	General Armand Philippon heads a French garrison against the British army under the command of the Duke of Wellington.
WHAT	At the third attempt the British were able to take the castle, after great valor on the part of both sides.
WHERE	Badajoz, Spain.
WHEN	April 6, 1812
WHY	Badajoz was one of the keys to Spain. The Allied army had to take it if they were to penetrate inland and on into southern France.
OUTCOME	Although the siege finally succeeded, the British infantry marred the achievement by indulging in a three-day orgy of rape, drunkenness and plunder against the local population.

The Duke of Wellington was a great general, but the sieges he led were not well handled. Badajoz was an example where, though he finally prevailed, it actually cost the lives of nearly 5000 soldiers in his command.

PENINSULAR WAR

ANGLO-PORTUGUESE VICTORY

The effort of the British 88th Foot in scaling the walls at Badajoz would be decisive to securing victory after attempts to breach the fortifications with gunfire had failed.

LOCATION

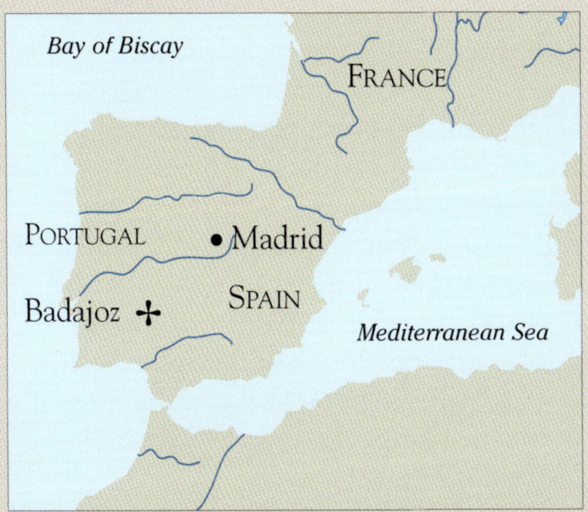

More sieges were conducted in Spain and Portugal between 1808 and 1814 than in any other theatre of war during the period.

The British twice had tried and failed to take Badajoz in the Peninsular War before a third attempt was made in the spring of 1812. The garrison of about 5000 men was ably commanded by the redoubtable General Armand Philippon, who had rendered it as difficult as possible to assail. Obstacles had been built in the ditch to render it unusable as a customary rallying place. Although the walls were breached, the defenders erected more obstacles within them and shored up the defenses.

SUCCESSFUL SIEGE

Major-General Thomas Picton's attack on the castle at first failed, and Picton himself was wounded. He rallied his men, however, and they gained a foothold on the lower walls. Scaling ladders were raised and the British poured over the parapet. Resistance was savage, but the British fought through adversity, taking the castle but with heavy casualties. General Philippon and the garrison withdrew into San Cristobal, where they surrendered the next day.

TIMELINE

1500–1000BC	1000–500BC	500BC–0AD	0–500AD	500–1000AD	1000–1500AD	1500–2000AD

Salamanca 1812

The Duke of Wellington was known as a sound commander, and a master of the defensive situation. At Salamanca, he was able to demonstrate that he could also orchestrate a brilliantly executed attack.

PENINSULAR WAR

BRITISH VICTORY

KEY FACTS

Who Arthur Wellesley (Duke of Wellington) leads the British army against Auguste Marmont in charge of the French and Anglo-Portuguese army.

What The British army, seemingly in retreat, were able to turn a cautious defensive position into an offensive and tear into a larger French army that had become overstretched.

Where Arapiles, Salamanca, Spain.

When July 22, 1812

Why Wellington and the British army were attempting to thwart French efforts to cement their control of Portugal and Spain.

Outcome Wellington was able to move on Madrid and take it back from the French.

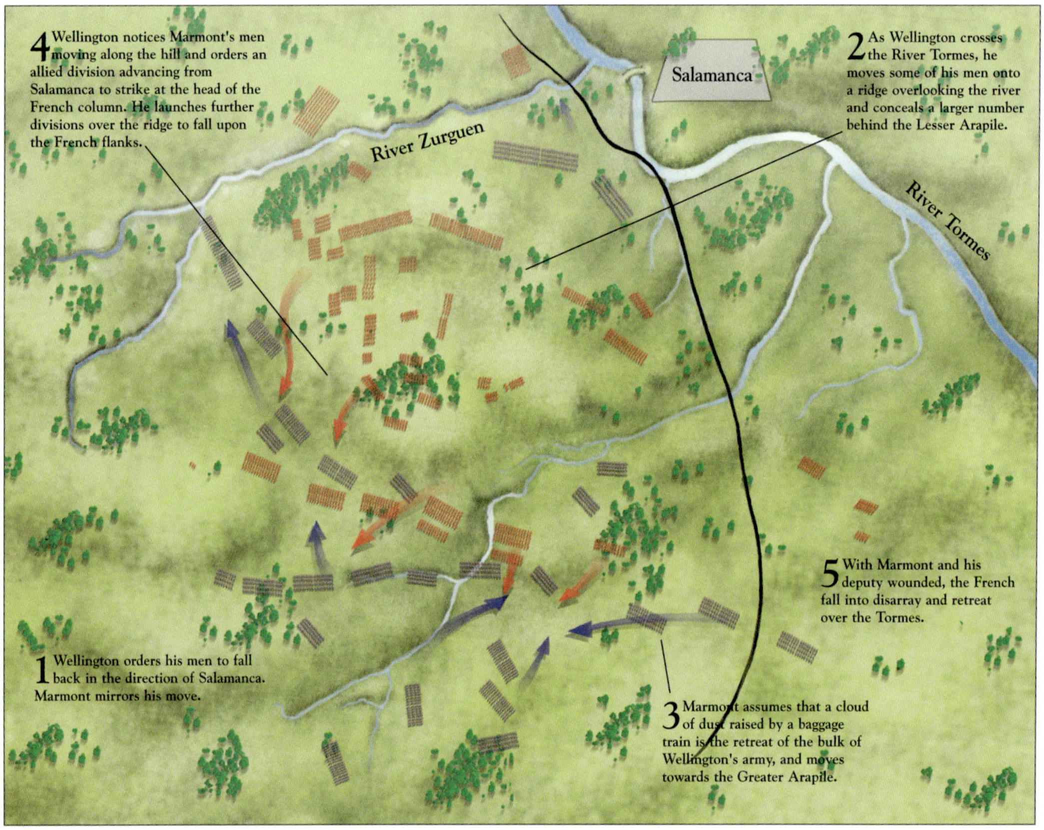

Salamanca has been dubbed "Wellington's masterpiece." Two years before his triumph at Waterloo, he was already revealing himself to be a tactical genius.

LOCATION

Salamanca stands in an area of sparse, rather monotonous plain, guarding routes that lead west toward the Portuguese frontier territory.

France, under Napoleon Bonaparte, had occupied Spain, overthrown the ruling Bourbon family and placed Napoleon's brother Joseph on the throne. The high-handed nature of the French occupation quickly stirred up local resentment, however, and a rebellious spirit spread across the entire Iberian peninsula. A British force under Sir John Moore was despatched to exploit the situation and save Portugal from being completely overrun. While Moore was successful in this objective, he lost his life and his army suffered heavy losses when it was pursued by the French and cornered at Coruna on the northern tip of Spain in 1809.

A new force under Arthur Wellesley, soon to be elevated to the peerage as the Duke of Wellington, was sent out to consolidate the hold on Portugal. A series of minor battles took place at fortresses along the Portuguese and Spanish frontier between the British and the French and these culminated in the Battle of Salamanca, often dubbed "Wellington's masterpiece."

Wellington had noted, with some concern, that the

Neither side especially desired a confrontation in the lead-up to the Battle of Salamanca, with the preceding days involving an element of "shadowing" as the two forces moved in close proximity through the plains near the city.

number of soldiers at the disposal of the French army under the command of Marshal Auguste Marmont appeared to be increasing, and so he had ordered his men to fall back in the direction of Salamanca. His move was mirrored by Marmont. The French commander was under pressure from Joseph Bonaparte to attack the British, but he was wary of getting engaged in a major battle. Wellington, too, was in a cautious mood, believing his army to be outnumbered, but he was prepared to wait for the circumstances to turn in his favor. As he crossed the River Tormes, nearing Salamanca, he moved some of his men onto a ridge overlooking the river, while moving a larger number behind a hill, the Lesser Arapile, effectively concealed from the view of the enemy.

Marmont, meanwhile, observing the British movements from a distance, saw a cloud of dust that was raised by a baggage train moving off towards Ciudad Rodrigo, but which he interpreted as a sign that the bulk of Wellington's army was in retreat, with merely the rearguard left to face him on the ridge. He determined on executing a south and then westwards maneuver along the side of the hill, the Greater Arapile, which ran parallel to the Lesser Arapile across the valley. His plan was to pin Wellington's army to its position, effectively cutting its communication lines with Portugal. However, as his men moved along the hill, Wellington noticed that the French divisions had become too strung out and that they had become exposed on the flanks.

QUICK THINKING

Spotting an opportunity, he rushed to meet a division under the control of his brother-in-law Edward Pakenham, which was advancing from Salamanca with the Portuguese cavalry, and ordered it to meet and strike at the head of the French advance column. He then launched further divisions over the ridge to fall upon the French flanks. Early on in the attack, Marmont himself and his deputy General Bonet were wounded by shrapnel fire, and in the absence of their command the French fell into disarray. While a measure of control was regained, overall recovery was impossible and those French who were not slaughtered left to beat a hasty retreat over the Tormes.

TIMELINE

1500–1000BC	1000–500BC	500BC–0AD	0–500AD	500–1000AD	1000–1500AD	1500–2000AD

Borodino 1812

KEY FACTS

Who The French Emperor Napoleon, leading some 130,000 men, opposed by a Russian army totalling around 120,000 men (including militia), commanded by Prince Mikhail Illarionovich Golenishchev-Kutuzov (1745–1813).

What The main French force was advancing on Moscow. After a series of attempts at resistance, the Russians established a defensive position at the village of Borodino.

Where The village of Borodino on the Moskowa River.

When September 7, 1812

Why The breakdown of the Treaty of Tilsit resulted in renewed war between Imperial Russia and Republican France. Napoleon hoped to force a new treaty on Russia.

Outcome A bloody and indecisive action. The French retained the battlefield and thus claimed victory. The advance on Moscow continued.

Napoleon had not intended to march so deep into Russia, but he was unable to force a decisive engagement, and was drawn onwards. Taking Moscow seemed to offer a way to end the campaign in victory. As the over-extended Grande Armée advanced, the defenders made a stand at Borodino.

NAPOLEONIC WARS

NO CLEAR VICTORY

The Russian success at Borodino—though not technically a win at all—was considered so significant it is celebrated as Russian Military Glory Day on its anniversary.

LOCATION

Borodino is a village along the Moskowa River astride the main highway to Moscow, which is roughly 50 miles (80 km) east of the village.

After the short-lived Treaty of Tilsit, Napoleon was soon at war again with Russia. But when his Grande Armée crossed the border, it was with supplies that were barely sufficient to maintain a short campaign—a state of affairs that was acceptable to the Emperor, who intended to win a decisive battle early on.

SUPPLY PROBLEMS

The ability of the French army to move rapidly was mostly due to its skill in foraging on the march and thus travelling light. This worked in the fertile countryside of central Europe, but in Russia there was little forage to be had. Its supply line was also subject to Russian attacks from the very beginning of the campaign, mostly by bands of fast-moving Cossacks who favored ambush attacks, using their lances and sabers. As the French supply line lengthened, the army gradually weakened to disease, accidents, harassment by irregular forces and straggling. The reduced capability of the French to fight played into the hands of the retreating commander of

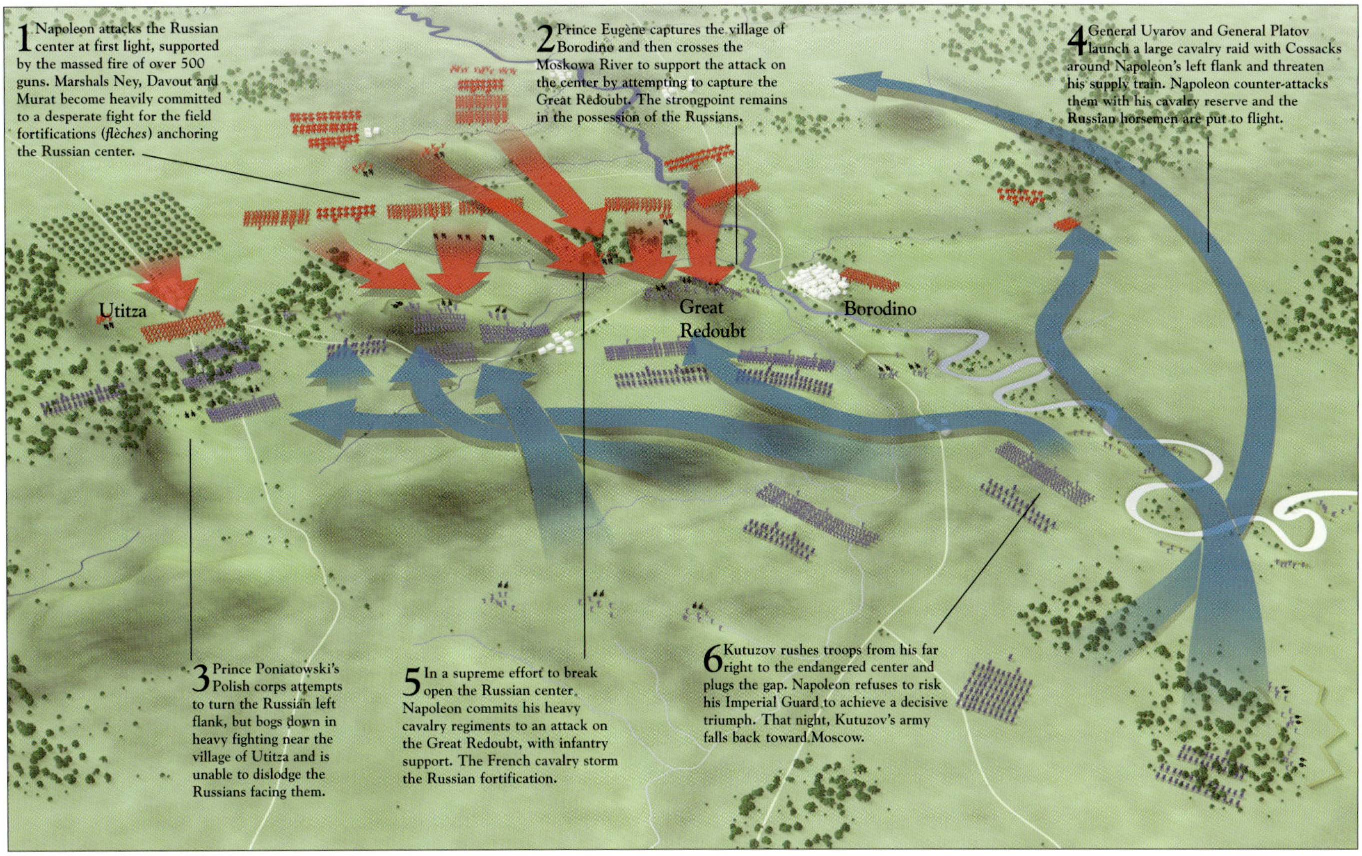

The Russian approach at Borodino was predicated on the assumption that Napoleon, after a long time in the field and on the march, with supplies under great strain, would want to come to battle as quickly as possible.

the Russian army Prince Mikhail Kutuzov, who set up a defensive position near Borodino, spanning the approach to Moscow.

Napoleon decided on a straightforward frontal attack, hoping to use the superior fighting power of his army to punch his way through the heavily defended Russian positions. To support this, he deployed a Grand Battery of 102 guns to face the main Russian positions at a series of earthworks known as *flèches* (after their arrowhead shape). Many of these guns were heavy 12-pounders capable of inflicting serious damage on the defenders, despite the protection of their earthworks. As the guns opened fire, the infantry advanced and were able to take control of the *flèches,* but then came under fire themselves from the Russian Imperial Guard and supporting elite Grenadier formations, with artillery support.

The greatest of the fortifications that strengthened the Russian line was the Great Redoubt, which the French, again using artillery fire, were able to force their way into and ultimately hold. However, it was only after a titanic effort that the French did so. A pause to reorganize and rest drew out into a gradual wind-down of the action, though the artillery of both sides continued to fire, and skirmishing took place all across the battlefield for some time.

INCONCLUSIVE OUTCOME

Although the defensive line had been broken and the Russians had been pushed back, they were not defeated in any real sense. Napoleon refused to commit the French Imperial Guard for one last push, perhaps because it was his only remaining reserve, so the Russians were able to retreat without pursuit. This left the French in possession of the battlefield, the traditional measure of victory. However, they had not in practice achieved any of their strategic aims. Both sides had lost 30,000–40,000 men, but, unlike the Russians on home soil, the French could not replace theirs. Strung out at the end of a long supply line, the French needed a decisive victory while the Russians only had to avoid total defeat. The Russians, although bloodied, had hurt the invaders badly, denying Napoleon the short campaign he had envisaged.

TIMELINE

1500–1000BC	1000–500BC	500BC–0AD	0–500AD	500–1000AD	1000–1500AD	1500–2000AD

Borodino

BORODINO

Many of Napoleon's battles involved severe numbers of casualties, but Borodino and its bloody aftermath could be described as a holocaust. Technically, since it was the Russians who withdrew from the Borodino battlefield, the day belonged to Napoleon's army, but his opponent's army, despite heavy casualties, was essentially intact, while his was adrift in a foreign land, weary and short of supplies. It has been estimated that Borodino, combined with the subsequent ignominious French retreat from Moscow in the thick of winter, resulted in around one million casualties, a horrid foretaste of the losses during World War I a century later.

Retreat from Moscow 1812

NAPOLEONIC WARS

RUSSIAN VICTORY

After what was a disputed victory at Borodino, Napoleon arrived in Moscow—the pinnacle of his Russian objective—to find a deserted city. Combined with the earlier slaughter on both sides, the losses sustained on the long march home meant this campaign had seen about a million lives lost.

KEY FACTS

WHO	The French Emperor Napoleon, and a Russian army commanded by Prince Mikhail Illarionovich Golenishchev-Kutuzov.
WHAT	Napoleon had to beat a retreat through a perishing Russian countryside in winter, his men starving, wracked by disease and assailed by fast moving Cossack light cavalrymen.
WHERE	Moscow, Russia.
WHEN	October–December 1812
WHY	Napoleon had invaded Russia, but entered Moscow to find merely a deserted, burnt-out city.
Outcome	Napoleon's magnificent Grande Armée had been virtually wiped out, and now France faced a group of enemies salivating for revenge.

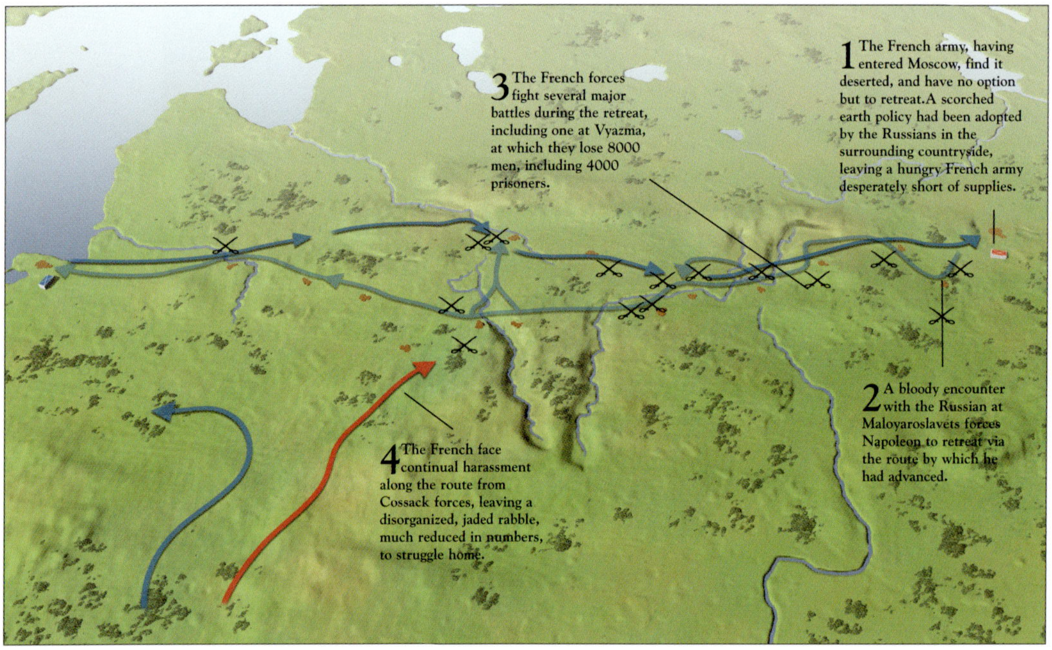

When the French arrived in Moscow they effectively found an empty city, denuded of the supplies and comforts they desperately craved after a long campaign and the draining encounter at Borodino.

After the ordeal at Borodino, Prince Mikhail Kutuzov realized that his army was in no condition to fight another battle. For his part, Napoleon took Moscow, but was effectively left in control of an empty city, with little to eat and no prospect of resupply. The only option was a retreat.

Returning via the same route as used for the advance seemed impractical, as this had been denuded of supplies by foraging, and a deliberate scorched earth policy by the Russians. But another bloody clash at Maloyaroslavets forced a rethink, and Napoleon had to retire along his original route of advance.

MAJOR CASUALTIES

Casualties during the Moscow Retreat were immense, from hunger, cold and on-going attacks by Russian forces, including continual harassment by the Cossack cavalry. In the end, only about 30,000–40,000 troops of the 630,000 that had entered Russia re-emerged in formed units. About the same number eventually straggled to safety, having endured unimaginable suffering.

LOCATION

Moscow was protected by both its distance from the European frontiers and by the harsh winter weather that descended upon the French troops.

TIMELINE

1500–1000BC	1000–500BC	500BC–0AD	0–500AD	500–1000AD	1000–1500AD	1500–2000AD

Hamburg 1813

KEY FACTS

Who	A French force under Marshal Davout's XIII Corps, against a Russian army under General Bennigsen.
What	Marshal Davout, under strict orders not to let the fortified city of Hamburg fall, put up a spirited defense, despite limiting provision before the final command came to submit.
Where	Hamburg, Germany.
When	December 1813–May 1814
Why	After defeat in Russia, France's enemies were attempting to regain ground. Hamburg was an important city that the French desperately wanted to retain.
Outcome	Having been the most successful defense of a fortified position during the Revolutionary and Napoleonic periods, Davout's valiant stand would be studied by professional soldiers for years to come.

Marshal Davout was a soldier with a distinguished record. At Auerstädt in 1806 and Eylau in 1807, he had played a distinguished part in two of the great French victories of the Napoleonic era. Now, as the curtain came down on Bonaparte's greatest years, there was time for one last stand.

NAPOLEONIC WARS

RUSSIAN-PRUSSIAN VICTORY

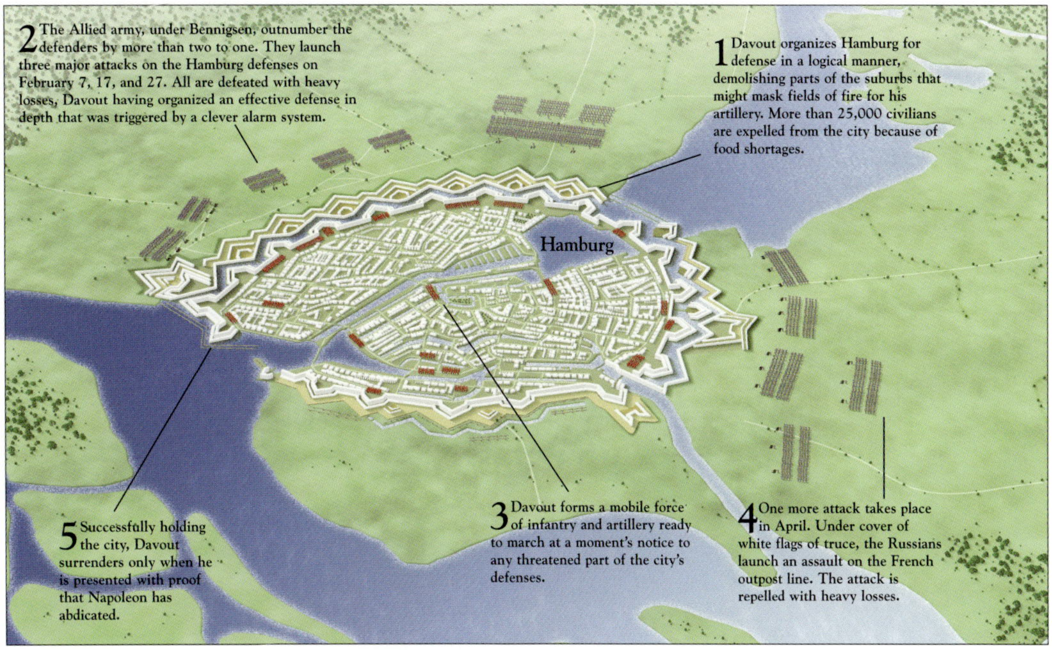

Marshal Davout was an experienced and loyal general, much respected in the French army. His defiant stand at Hamburg came in the dying years of the Napoleonic era.

Marshal Davout was tasked with holding Hamburg as the Russian-Prussian alliance fought back after Napoleon's Moscow debacle. By the time a siege began, Davout was increasingly isolated. With no news from the main army, he could only assume he was on his own.

Davout had taken every precaution to defend the city to the last. Neglected defenses had been improved, and civilians were warned to start storing food for a siege. Russian General Bennigsen's forces outnumbered Davout's by more than two to one, yet three major attacks on the Hamburg defenses were all defeated.

DEFIANT STAND

Bennigsen settled down to starve his opponent into submission. One more attack took place when, under cover of white flags of truce, the Russians launched an assault on the French outpost line. The French, however, were ready and neatly repelled the Russians, sending them back to their lines with heavy losses. At last, word came that Napoleon had abdicated in April. Davout, defiant to the end, refused to surrender until he was ordered to by competent French authority.

LOCATION

Hamburg is a strategic port city on the lower Elbe, which Napoleon considered vital to hold. Consequently, Marshal Davout was tasked with its defense.

TIMELINE

1500–1000BC	1000–500BC	500BC–0AD	0–500AD	500–1000AD	1000–1500AD	1500–2000AD

Lake Erie 1813

KEY FACTS

WHO British naval squadron under Commander Robert Heriot Barclay against American soldiers and sailors led by Lieutenant Jesse Elliot and Master Commandant Oliver Hazard Perry.

WHAT An increasingly confident American navy cornered and destroyed a small squadron of British ships, thanks in part to the resourceful leadership of its commander.

WHERE Lake Erie, near Put-in-Bay, Ohio.

WHEN September 10, 1813

WHY The US had declared war on Britain after the latter had blockaded her trade ships from Continental Europe.

OUTCOME The British lost control of Lake Erie, and the American victory was a massive boost to the morale of its increasingly confident navy.

While the big beasts of France, Prussia, Russia and Austria thundered around on the European stage, slowly a fledgling nation across the Atlantic was starting to flap its wings. In 1813, the United States was still a minor player, but it was being taken increasingly seriously.

WAR OF 1812

US VICTORY

Oliver Hazard Perry, the master commandant who led the American fleet to victory at Lake Erie, was forced to abandon his flagship at one stage of the fighting.

LOCATION

Control of the Great Lakes and the St. Lawrence River was vital for the successful defense and attack ambitions of both the United States and Canada.

Just 30 years old, the group of Great Britain's tiny former colonies now known as the United States of America had set itself on a course of expansion with minimum pretext. The United States attacked and conquered additional territory from the southern Native Americans and amongst the Spanish colonies of Florida and Miami. It negotiated the purchase of New Orleans from France and turned its avaricious gaze northwards to Canada. True, here there was some provocation. Britain had been mounting an effective blockade of Continental Europe, with whom the United States wanted to trade. Also, US merchantmen had been stopped and searched by the Royal Navy, looking for seamen deserters.

Frustrated by the British blockade, President James Madison (1751–1836) declared war and ordered the US Navy to build squadrons to wrest naval superiority from the British. Super-strong frigates would be built to a standard normally reserved for line of battle ships. These would challenge such ships as could be isolated from the British fleet.

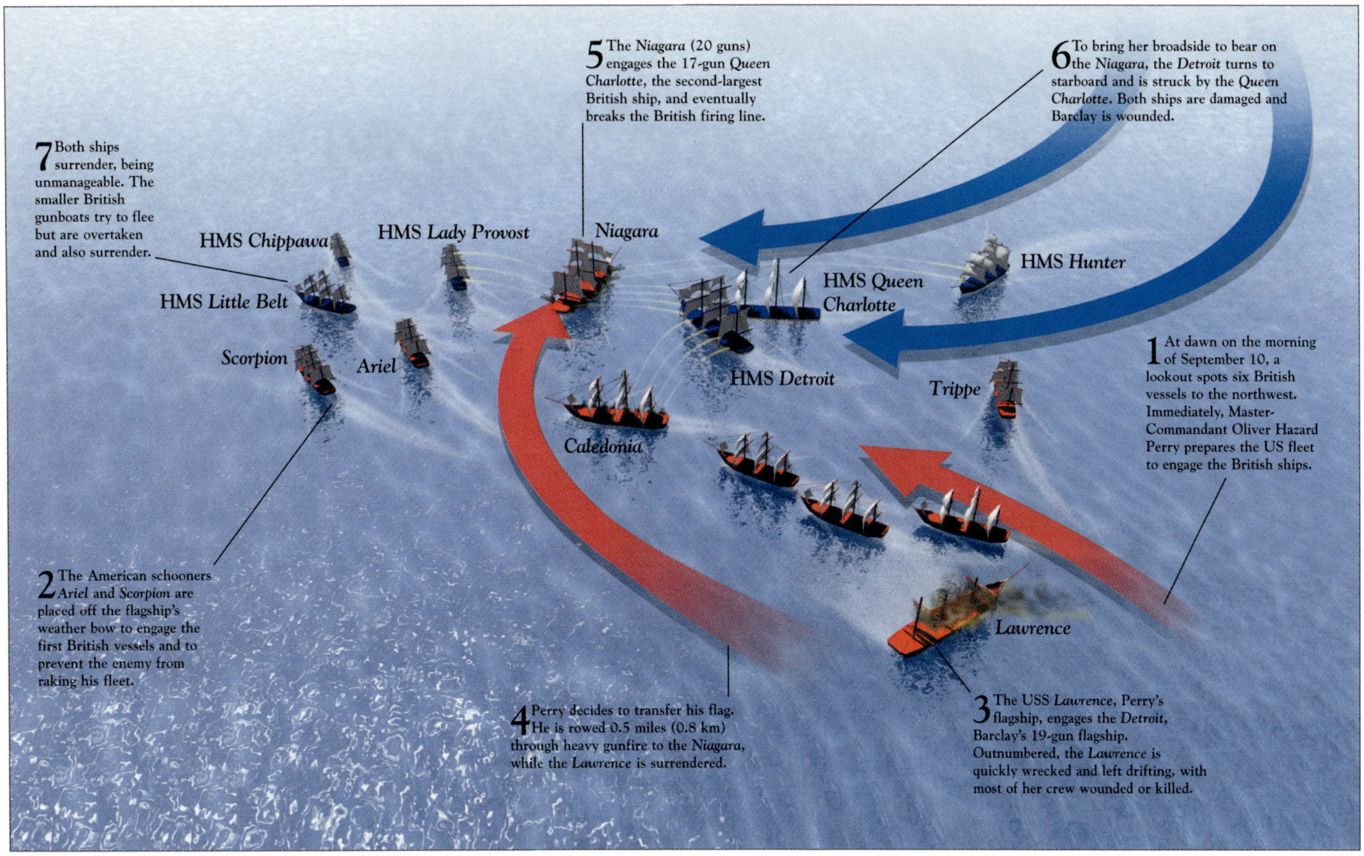

The fighting on Lake Erie began with the Americans cruising off the Detroit River, in what proved to be a successful attempt to provoke a response from the British flotilla. The American vessels had the advantage of superior numbers and, eventually, favorable winds.

A small new force, comprising the *Oneida* and six adapted lake ships, was ready on November 8, 1812. The force chased but did not catch two British ships. As winter closed in, both sides directed their energies to their shipyards and built more vessels. The British responded by constructing a 30-gun frigate and two corvettes and transferring 450 experienced sailors from the Royal Navy.

The Americans pressed ahead with building a new corvette, the 24-gun Madison, modifying the *Lady of the Lake* and starting work on their own frigate of 26 guns. Both sides also equipped several sail- and oar-powered launches with a single gun in the bows. By August 1813 both sides were ready to begin operations. Large parts of the US–Canadian border passed through the Great Lakes area, and here some of the major action took place. The forces again involved consisted of small ships carrying small guns.

The Americans and the British now had squadrons of warships on both Lake Ontario and Lake Erie. The American commander, Master-Commandant Oliver Hazard Perry (1785–1819) began by cruising off the Detroit River, trying to provoke a response from the British flotilla. It eventually had the desired effect. The British emerged on September 10, with a favorable breeze, and their two lead ships concentrated on the *Lawrence*, Perry's flagship. The next in the American line, the *Caledonia*, was lagging behind. Within just a few minutes, the American *Lawrence* was a wreck, with two-thirds of her crew casualties.

Perry got himself rowed over to the *Niagara* to continue the battle. However, the British officer corps was suffering badly from the American gunnery. *Detroit*, *Queen Charlotte*, *Hunter* and *Prevost* all lost their first lieutenants, and the British commander-in-chief was also mortally wounded. As the British attempted to sort themselves out, Perry charged his ship into their line, firing broadsides in both directions. The *Detroit* attempted to turn downwind to bring her broadside to bear but was run into by the *Queen Charlotte*, which had not responded similarly. This was clearly a mess, and with eight US ships in the immediate vicinity compared with four serviceable vessels in the British flotilla, the latter surrendered.

TIMELINE

1500–1000BC	1000–500BC	500BC–0AD	0–500AD	500–1000AD	1000–1500AD	1500–2000AD

Leipzig 1813

KEY FACTS

WHO	French army of Napoleon and his allies, against the Sixth Coalition, including Russia, Prussia, Austria, Sweden and Saxony.
WHAT	After three days of close fighting, with heavy casualties on both sides, Napoleon was forced to stage a planned retreat.
WHERE	Leipzig, Germany.
WHEN	October 16–19, 1813
WHY	A grand Coalition of European nations had formed against the empire of Napoleon Bonaparte.
OUTCOME	Napoleon had lost a major part of his army, and all of his German territories.

The Battle of Leipzig was a catastrophic defeat for the once ascendant Napoleon. His defeat in Germany against a large coalition army led to the Allied invasion of France itself, and to Napoleon's abdication and temporary exile to the island of Elba in the Mediterranean.

NAPOLEONIC WARS

SIXTH COALITION VICTORY

The Battle of Leipzig took place within view of the Baroque towers of the historic German city and cost the combatants more than 100,000 casualties.

LOCATION

An empire that took seven years to build collapsed in central Germany in a climactic three-day battle. It remained the largest engagement in Europe until 1866.

By October 1813, Napoleon was under attack from Allied armies closing in from the north and south, so he withdrew his army to Leipzig, closer to his Rhenish allies, to prepare for battle.

Leipzig differed from previous Napoleonic battles in that the emperor's enemies coordinated their operations and cooperated effectively. Also known as the "Battle of the Nations," it was the largest battle fought in Europe until the wars of German unification of 1866 and 1870–71. Almost half a million soldiers from more than a dozen European states were engaged during the three days of fighting. In the end, Napoleon lost a large part of his army, and all of Germany.

Napoleon intended to attack Schwarzenberg's Austrian army while keeping Blücher's Prussians at bay, but neither man intended to pass the initiative to the Frenchman. The Austrian field marshal was well aware that he faced the bulk of Napoleon's army. Confident that he could bring greater numbers to bear, Schwarzenberg ordered a general advance, hoping to turn Napoleon's flank to the east while

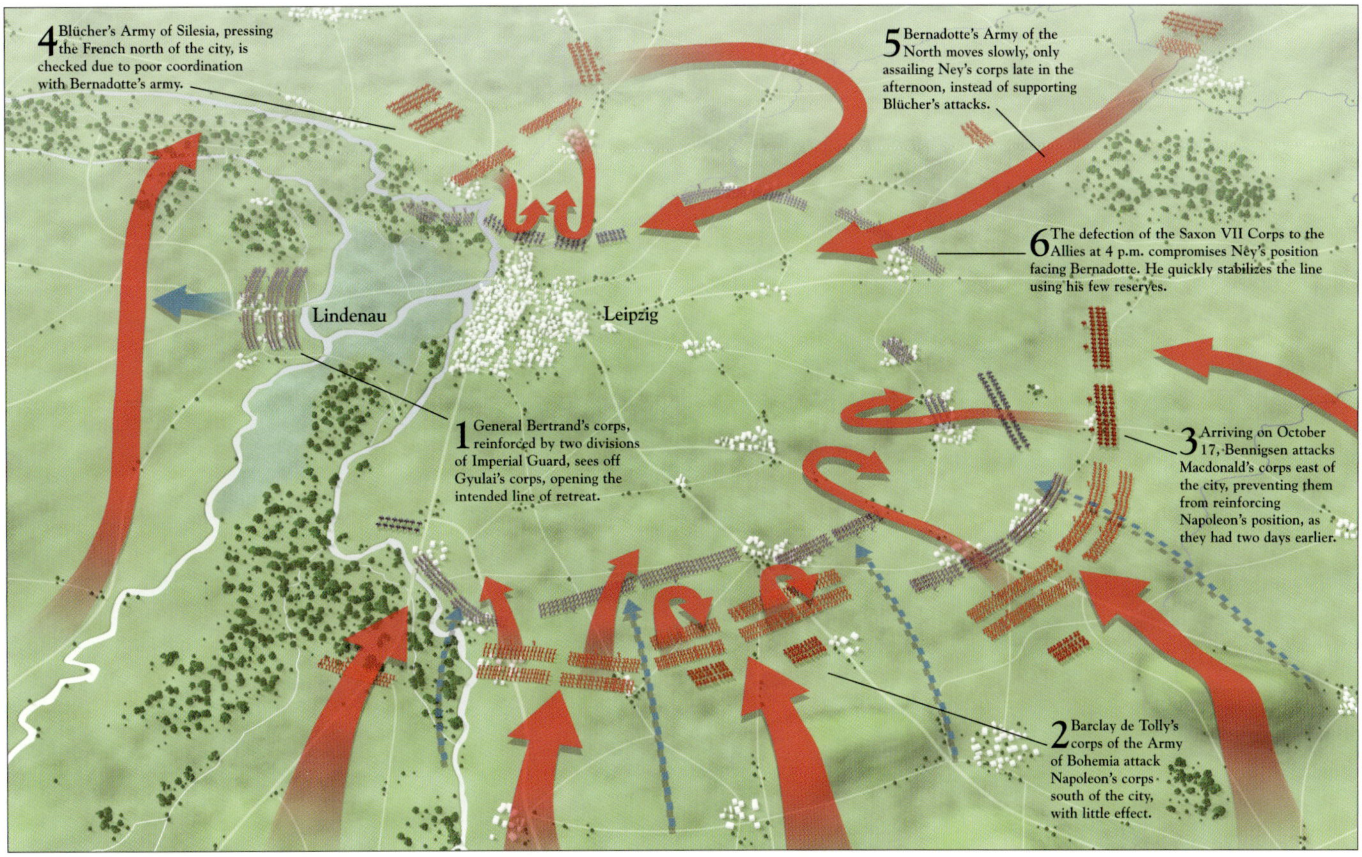

At Leipzig, Napoleon knew that defeat in the battle would mean the collapse of his ambitions in central Europe. His attempt to stage a managed withdrawal to stave off the worst of the consequences proved unsuccessful.

he pinned the larger part of the French Army south of the city. Blücher was to vigorously attack Leipzig from the north, preventing the French corps in that vicinity from moving to support Napoleon. To complete the destruction of the French imperial army, Schwarzenberg dispatched Count Ignaz Gyulai's Austrian corps west of the Elster, with Lindenau and Napoleon's line of retreat as its objective.

The fighting began with an advance of Russian and Prussians under General Ludwig Wittgenstein, but the fire from Napoleon's massed heavy batteries was so intense that no advantage was gained, and after two hours of fighting the French launched a counter-attack. Although Napoleon's attack on the enemy center met with some success, nightfall and exhaustion meant decisive victory eluded his men.

After a day of recuperation, Napoleon's position grew more precarious with the arrival of Bernadotte's Swedish troops to bolster Allied ranks, and Blücher pushed the French back towards the city. While Napoleon understood that wholesale withdrawal would provide the Allies with a tremendous victory and no doubt lead to the collapse of his empire in Germany, he began to prepare for a general retreat, hoping his army would wound the Allies before escaping towards the Rhine.

After a day of combat, night fell without the Allies having reached the city. Napoleon's luck had held, but he knew it would not do so for much longer. He ordered a phased withdrawal of corps through the city and across the Elster river. Engineers were given orders to blow charges on the bridge once the army was across. On October 18, they began to move to the west bank of the Elster. The Allies launched attacks into the city's suburbs, reaching the walls by late morning. Hard fighting around the city gates continued until 1 p.m., prematurely destroying the bridge. More than 30,000 French and imperial troops were trapped in Leipzig. With Napoleon leading his army away to the west, the defenders surrendered.

Leipzig was a tremendous coalition victory at a heavy price. Napoleon suffered 70,000 killed, wounded or taken prisoner. The Allies lost 54,000 men. Despite this, the Allies had succeeded in bringing their armies together in overwhelming numbers, producing a strategic victory.

TIMELINE

1500–1000BC	1000–500BC	500BC–0AD	0–500AD	500–1000AD	1000–1500AD	1500–2000AD

Leipzig

LEIPZIG

By 1813, Napoleon was running out of time, no longer the "lucky general" of yesteryear. Other European powers, of course, had long since sickened of his deeds, but now they bound themselves together to form a massive coalition of a dozen states, including Russia, Prussia, Austria, Sweden and Saxony. Altogether, around half a million men would be involved in three days of fighting at Leipzig, the greatest battle of the era when horses took their place alongside muskets on the battlefield. Both sides lost large numbers of men, but it was the aging Napoleon who suffered the severest dent to his standing.

Lützen 1813

KEY FACTS

WHO Napoleon Bonaparte and the French Army against the Allied Forces of Prussia and Russia under Count von Blücher.

WHAT A spectacular artillery attack blew a hole in the Allied forces' center, paving the way for Napoleon himself to lead a decisive infantry assault.

WHERE Near Lützen, Germany.

WHEN May 2, 1813.

WHY Napoleon had rebuilt his Grande Armée after it was crushed at Borodino and was desperate to repel the newly confident alliance of Prussia and Russia.

OUTCOME Napoleon had shown he still had teeth, but further challenges lay ahead.

After Napoleon's disastrous Russian campaign, the momentum seemed now to lie with his enemies. Their foe, however, was desperate not to concede much further ground. An unexpected encounter at Lützen showed there was life in the French lion yet.

NAPOLEONIC WARS

FRENCH VICTORY

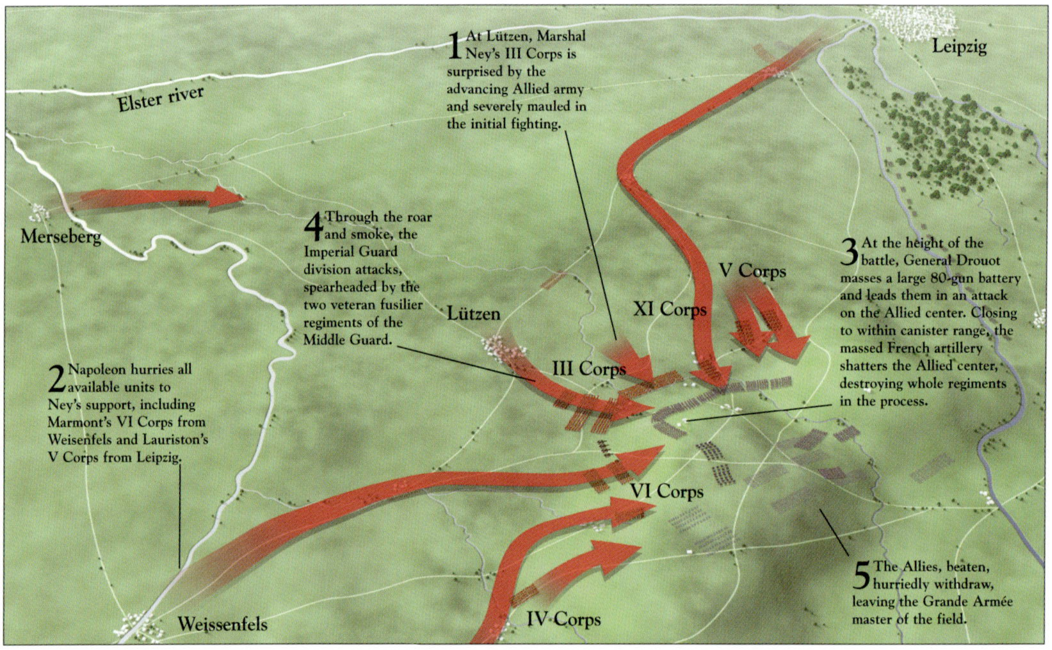

The fighting at Lutzen included some spectacular artillery fire from both sides. While this was one of Napoleon's last victories, his troops were so exhausted they were unable to finish off their opponents.

After his disastrous Russian campaign, Napoleon rebuilt the shattered Grande Armée and by April 1813 was advancing into Germany to link up with Prince Eugène's Army of the Elbe. The new Grande Armée was numerically superior to its Allied antagonists, but except for the Imperial Guard, the army was in large part made up of new conscripts with less than a year's service and therefore experience.

LOCATION

Lützen, near Leipzig in Saxony, was the site of the first large battle of the 1813 campaign. The Allies, though achieving surprise, were thoroughly beaten.

ARTILLERY STRIKE

Count von Blücher's army caught Napoleon by surprise near Lützen, but spectacular artillery action led by General Drouot turned the action in the French favor. Drouot organized and led forward 80 artillery pieces from the Imperial Guard and line artillery. Massed within canister range of the Allied center, these literally blew a hole in the Allied line and paved the way for the decisive infantry assault by the Guard infantry, led by Napoleon. Whole Allied infantry regiments were destroyed, covering the ground with dead and wounded. However, because the French were shattered from their earlier march, the Allies were able to withdraw from the battlefield in good order.

TIMELINE

1500–1000BC	1000–500BC	500BC–0AD	0–500AD	500–1000AD	1000–1500AD	1500–2000AD

Quatre Bras 1815

KEY FACTS

Who A contingent of the French led by Marshal Ney against the British led by the Duke of Wellington.

What A critical delay by Marshal Ney, concerned not to encounter the full might of the Anglo-Dutch army, allowed a rushed Wellington more time to deploy and avoid defeat.

Where Crossroads of Quartre Bras, modern Belgium.

When June 16, 1815

Why The French needed to obstruct the Anglo-Dutch and Prussian forces linking up, and Quatre Bras was a strategically vital crossroads.

Outcome Wellington withdrew towards Waterloo, for his showdown with Napoleon.

In the Hundred Days War, Napoleon faced an offensive on two fronts, so he divided his Armée du Nord in two. While he dealt with the Prussians, it fell to Marshal Michel Ney to deal with Wellington and his allies.

NAPOLEONIC WARS

NO CLEAR VICTORY

Quatre Bras was a bitterly contested battle which ended in a draw. The French cavalry attacks led by Marshal Ney were undermined by poor coordination.

LOCATION

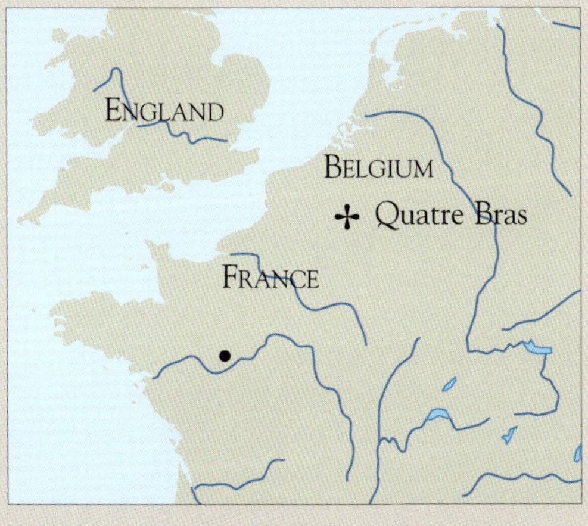

Quatre Bras was a tiny hamlet in southern Belgium located at a vital crossroads of the main highway to Brussels some 25 miles (40 km) to the north.

Napoleon had ordered Marshal Ney to take possession of the key crossroads of Quatre Bras. Ney moved cautiously forward, fearful of encountering the Duke of Wellington's main Anglo–Allied Army. However, this meant Wellington was able to rush to the scene of action, and deploy his forces to give stubborn resistance. Ney's position was further weakened when Comte d'Erlon's corps were called by Napoleon to support the main French army, engaged in a concurrent battle with the Prussians at Ligny.

Napoleon also ordered Ney to speed his capture of Quatre Bras in order to fall upon the Prussian rear. A furious Ney hurled his cavalry forward in a desperate attempt to smash the Anglo–Allied forces. With reinforcements arriving steadily, Wellington repulsed Ney's attack and, by early evening, the French were outnumbered. Wellington counter-attacked, driving Ney's forces back to their original starting positions, though the battle ended in a draw. Wellington withdrew from the field the next day, retreating to fight the decisive Battle of Waterloo.

TIMELINE

1500–1000BC	1000–500BC	500BC–0AD	0–500AD	500–1000AD	1000–1500AD	1500–2000AD

Waterloo 1815

KEY FACTS

Who British, German, Belgian and Dutch allies, led by the Duke of Wellington, plus 50,000 Prussian troops under Marshal Blücher, against Napoleon's reformed French army.

What Napoleon resolved to attack the Allied forces before other powers could come to their aid.

Where Approximately 3 miles (5 km) south of the village of Waterloo, 8 miles (13 km) south of Brussels.

When June 18, 1815

Why In 1814, 25 years of European war ended and the major European powers started restoring their countries to normality. Napoleon's return from Elba threatened to jeopardize this.

Outcome The Quadruple Alliance, signed by those who fought at Waterloo, was designed to protect the balance of power.

A series of defeats for Napoleon Bonaparte (1769–1821) led to his exile on the island of Elba. However, he escaped back to France, reassembled his army and crossed the French border, intending to prevent an Allied invasion. Allied forces retaliated, bringing about his decisive defeat at Waterloo.

NAPOLEONIC WARS

BRITISH AND ALLIED VICTORY

The chateau of Hougoumont was the focal point of French attacks at Waterloo, a miscalculation by Napoleon, since it drew his troops away from the British center.

LOCATION

The Hundred Days campaign culminated with two of the most famous and successful generals of the age locked in battle at Waterloo.

When Napoleon escaped exile on Elba in 1815, he returned to France to remobilize the army, and move on Brussels. Wellington, at the head of the Allies, and the Prussian army under Marshal Gebherd von Blücher, were mobilized to meet him.

At Ligny, Napoleon was able to defeat Blücher's army, but it was not a killer blow, and the Prussians were able to retreat and, critically, join up with Wellington's army at Waterloo, some 8 miles (13 km) south of Brussels.

The Waterloo battle was to be fought over terrain comprising a network of small roads, orchards and farms. The center of action chosen by Wellington lay in the valley situated in front of the right wing of his front line. This was the château of Hougoumont Farm. Two other farms in the valley played a crucial role—Germans troops occupied La Haye Sainte and the French appropriated the nearby La Belle Alliance as their headquarters.

The battle began with a French attack on the chateau at Hougoument Farm, with Napoleon calling on howitzers to shell the château, which caught fire. Then Marshal

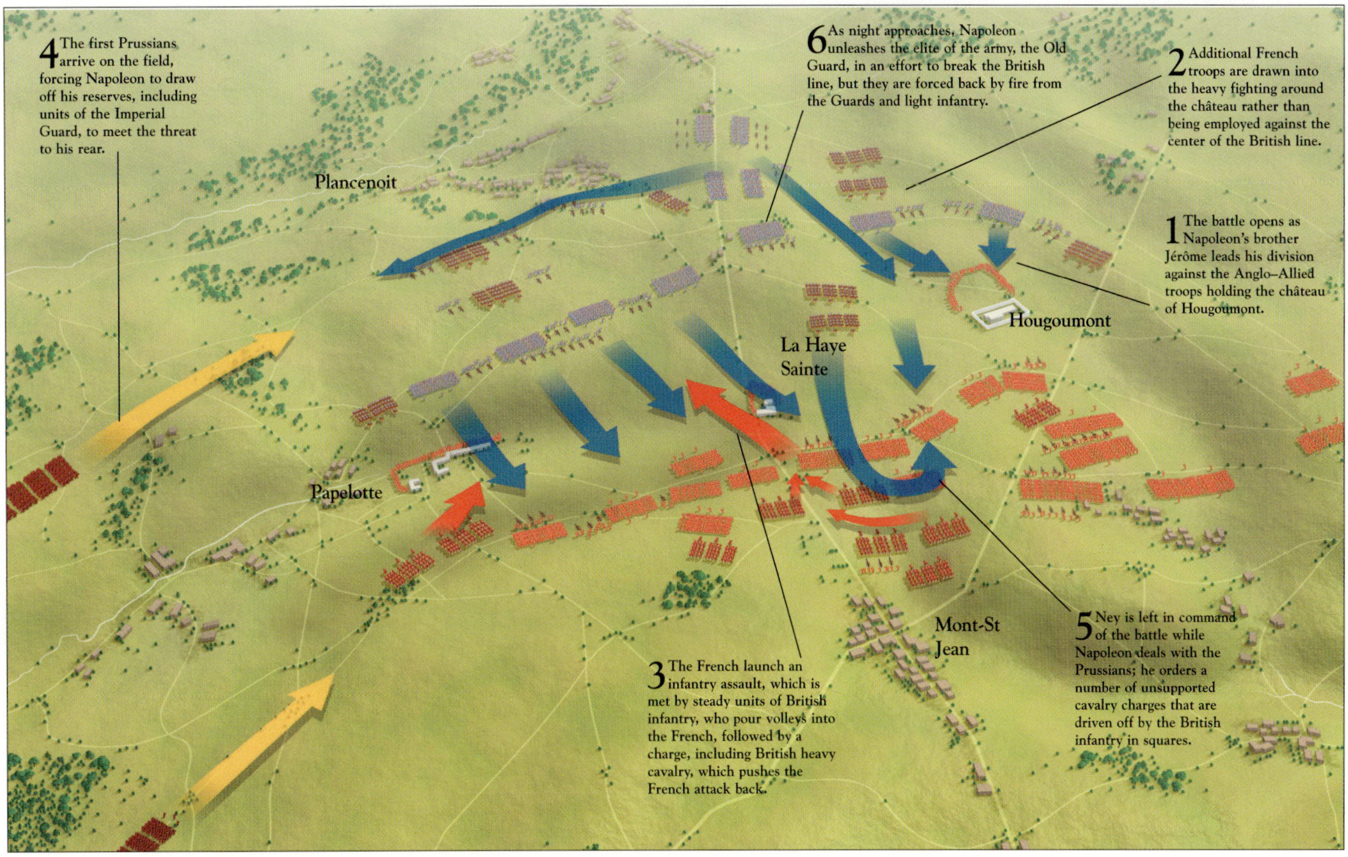

Waterloo was fought in difficult terrain for combat: a sleepy countryside of hedgerows, narrow lanes, small farms, and orchards. These features, however, would play important roles in defining the course of the battle.

Michel Ney, one of Napoleon's most trusted aides, brought forward 74 French guns over the ridge opposite La Haye Sainte, followed by 17,000 infantry, to start the attack on Wellington's center and left.

The effect of the French cannonade was partly lessened by an order from Wellington that his infantry battalions should move behind the ridge and lie down for protection, shielding them from the worst of enemy fire. As the French troops under Ney approached the top of the ridge, they were greeted with a fierce volley and a bayonet charge from the infantry division lead by General Sir Thomas Picton.

The French suffered a major setback when Ney thought he saw signs of Allied withdrawals, and led his attacking force of Cuirassiers cavalry—men equipped with helmets and breast plates—in a series of charges. But the Allied army, far from having withdrawn, had formed into squares interlaced with artillery barriers, which created a solid defensive position that the exhausted French troops could not overcome, leaving the slope littered with Ney's troopers.

Things got worse with the delayed arrival of Blücher's army, slowed by heavy rain in the approaching network of boggy, narrow lanes. While Ney pleaded for more troops to attack the enemy center, Napoleon concentrated on keeping Wellington's and Blücher's troops apart. By deploying his Young Guard on the Prussians, he gave Wellington time to regroup, and Ney's chance of pressing home a decisive attack had gone.

Late in the day, Napoleon led out the Old and Middle Guards, but it soon collided with the men of the British Brigade of Foot Guards, urged on by Wellington, who commanded, "Up Guards, ready." The Foot Guards fired a volley and charged with their bayonets, forcing the French Guard back. It took 15 minutes for Wellington to appear on the skyline and wave his hat, giving the signal for the all-out pursuit of the retreating French, and a mêlée of Allied forces quickly attacked. The French retreat became a rout. Three battalions of the Old Guard hung on to enable the Emperor to escape. He made no attempt to stay and rally his soldiers or conduct their retreat, but rode for his life. The Battle of Waterloo was over.

TIMELINE

1500–1000BC	1000–500BC	500BC–0AD	0–500AD	500–1000AD	1000–1500AD	1500–2000AD

Glossary

artillery Projectile or ranged weapons, such as bows, slings, and catapults, for discharging missiles.

cavalry A part of an army riding on horseback.

flank The right and left sides of a formation in an army, often vulnerable to attack. The term is also a verb in this meaning, to "flank" someone or something.

frigates Sailing warships built for speed while heavily armed on one or two decks.

Hundred Days The period between Napoleon returning to France to march with his soldiers on Paris to when King Louis XVIII returned to Paris and was restored.

infantry Soldiers trained, armed, and equipped to fight on foot.

megalomaniac A person who is obsessed with power, often to the point of considering themself omnipotent and above all others.

musket A smooth-bored, long-barreled, muzzleloading gun carried by an infantryman, fired from the shoulder, in part, because of its weight.

regiments Military units consisting of a number of battalions, or several large groups of soldiers.

rout When troops are forced into a disorganized retreat.

Further Reading

Dawson, Paul. *Marshal Ney At Quatre Bras: New Perspectives on the Opening Battle of the Waterloo Campaign.* Barnsley, UK: Frontline Books, 2017.

DK Publishing. *The American Revolution: A Visual History.* New York, NY: Author, 2016.

Harris, Michael C. *Brandywine: A Military History of the Battle that Lost Philadelphia but Saved America, September 11, 1777*. El Dorado Hills, CA: Savas Beatie, LLC., 2014.

Randall, Willard Sterne. *Unshackling America: How the War of 1812 Truly Ended the American Revolution*. New York, NY: St. Martin's Press, 2017.

Wells, Colin. *Poetry Wars: Verse and Politics in the American Revolution and Early Republic.* (Early American Studies.) Philadelphia, PA: University of Pennsylvania Press, 2017.

Websites

American Revolution
http://www.history.com/topics/american-revolution
The History Channel's website contains an archive of videos related to the American Revolution, along with links to articles on key figures and events in the war and infographics.

French Revolutionary Wars
https://www.britannica.com/event/French-revolutionary-wars
Encyclopædia Britannica provides an overview of the French Revolutionary Wars in this article, describing the key causes of the wars, where the wars fit into the broader European historical context, and key campaigns and events.

Revolt! Comparing Historical Revolutions
The *New York Times* provides this resource for teachers, which offers activities and questions for exploring key concepts related to historical revolutions. The site also provides links to primary and secondary sources on revolutions ranging from the American Revolution to the Nicaraguan Revolution of 1979.

Index